English as an Additional L
in the Early Years

With the English as an Additional Language (EAL) population growing rapidly, it is essential that educational settings meet individual learner needs and provide an inclusive environment where different languages, cultures and religions are accepted and celebrated. Packed with essential information on key theories and best practice, and written in a highly readable style, this book aims to raise awareness of the main issues and offer practical support for practitioners working with learners with EAL.

Covering a wide range of topics such as new arrivals, working with parents, assessment, planning, resourcing, play, communication and language, each chapter clearly lays out the key concepts, ideas and strategies alongside examples of good practice. Encouraging a reflective approach, the book features:

- checklists, diagrams, chapter objectives and summaries, and suggestions for further reading;
- case studies to illustrate practice;
- reflective activities to develop critical thinking.

Challenging many assumptions and stereotypes about EAL learners, this invaluable text will support students and practitioners in meeting the individual needs of all learners in their care.

Malini Mistry is Senior Lecturer in Early Years Education at the University of Bedfordshire with research interests in Early Years and learners who have English as an Additional Language.

Krishan Sood is Senior Lecturer at Nottingham Trent University with research interests in Leadership for Diversity and English as an Additional Language.

English as an Additional Language in the Early Years

Linking theory to practice

Malini Mistry and Krishan Sood

Routledge
Taylor & Francis Group

LONDON AND NEW YORK

First published 2015
by Routledge
2 Park Square, Milton Park, Abingdon, Oxon OX14 4RN

and by Routledge
711 Third Avenue, New York, NY 10017

Routledge is an imprint of the Taylor & Francis Group, an informa business

British Library Cataloguing in Publication Data
A catalogue record for this book is available from the British Library

Library of Congress Cataloging in Publication Data
Mistry, Malini.
English as an additional language in the early years: linking theory to practice/
Malini Mistry and Krishan Sood.
pages cm
Includes bibliographical references and index.
1. Bilingualism in children. 2. Second language acquisition. 3. English language—Study and teaching (Early childhood)—Foreign speakers. I. Sood, Krishan. II. Title.
P115.2.M57 2015
404'.2083—dc23
2014038107

ISBN: 978-0-415-82170-4 (hbk)
ISBN: 978-0-415-82171-1 (pbk)
ISBN: 978-0-203-55914-7 (ebk)

Typeset in Bembo
by Swales & Willis Ltd, Exeter, Devon, UK

Printed and bound in Great Britain by
TJ International Ltd, Padstow, Cornwall

Contents

Figures

Tables

Acknowledgements

'Life is a song – sing it. Life is a game – play it. Life is a challenge – meet it. Life is a dream – realize it. Life is a sacrifice – offer it. Life is love – enjoy it.'

Sri Sathya Sai Baba (Brainy quote, 2013: Online)

This book is inspired by our fantastic learners in Early Years settings, practitioners, colleagues and friends. A huge thank you to all of them for their encouragement and belief in our ideas. Also a special thanks to our editor Annamarie for her insightful ideas, feedback on the improvement of each chapter and her belief in us to showcase our ideas from our personal and professional experiences.

A very special thank you to our critical readers, respective universities and immediate families for their constant unconditional support, encouragement and endless cups of chai!

We would like to dedicate this book to all the learners, practitioners, parents, students and settings that helped us to inform and shape our thoughts. As a result, we too have grown in our own beliefs and values that have informed our thinking, writing and practice. We hope the book also shapes and improves the knowledge, understanding and reflective practice of the readers.

Setting the scene

'Education is the most powerful weapon which you can use to change the world.'
Nelson Mandela (Stutman, 2013)

The aims of this chapter

- To be aware of the changing educational landscape in meeting the needs of learners with EAL in the context of Early Years
- To explore how key policies and legislation have an impact on the needs of learners with EAL in Early Years

Overview

This book is about highlighting and sharing good practice that develops fresh perspectives on how best to meet the educational needs of learners with English as an Additional Language (EAL) in Early Years settings. It explores issues such as EAL learners' needs, working with parents of learners with EAL, assessment opportunities for learners with EAL and the resources needed for effective learning experiences among learners with EAL. The book is aimed at all trainees and practitioners working in the Early Years sector, higher education institutions, tutors and integrated children's services practitioners. We hope that it gives an accessible introduction to research and practice about learners with EAL, and goes some way in providing that varied knowledge and understanding to be reflexive, and also offers some practical ideas to those who are working with isolated EAL learners. The thrust behind writing this book came from our experiences as multilingual practitioners ourselves.

The focus of this book

We believe that this is the first book of its type that focuses on the cultural and social aspects of learners with EAL in the context of Early Years education in England. It is our vision that the next generations of Early Years practitioners should be more knowledgeable, confident and competent about the cultural and linguistic needs of learners with EAL, and therefore be better prepared to challenge misconceptions and misunderstandings about their needs.

As the focus of this book is on learners with EAL in the Early Years sector, we shall briefly look at the policy context and the implication of various acts and documentations as these have an impact on practice for these learners. The aim of this introductory chapter is to consider the key current policy drivers, to contextualise the issues and to highlight their impact on the learners with EAL within this fast-changing educational context. We next present a brief contextual review of the changing educational landscape that may have an impact on learners with EAL.

The changing landscape for supporting learners with EAL

According to the 2008 school census by NALDIC (National Association for Language Development in the Curriculum) there was a 25 per cent increase in numbers of learners with EAL from 2004 to 2008 in England's educational settings. Our research suggests that many practitioners are keenly looking to improve their knowledge and understanding of the cultural background of EAL learners and their families in order to help meet the educational needs of these learners more precisely to help raise standards. With increasing social mobility and expanding immigration patterns, many Early Years settings are grappling with providing a more inclusive culture to maximise their ability to match learner needs based on an expanding repertoire of languages and cultures. Such settings probably feel overwhelmed and quite understandably believe that learners whose first language is not English may be treated initially as if they have special educational needs. This book raises issues and challenges of such misconceptions about the needs of learners with EAL. As Conteh (2012: 1) highlights, it is important that practitioners look 'positively on diversity . . . for all children'.

Changing scenes, changing challenges

A changing, diverse learner population in England, especially in the urban regions, has brought with it the demand for different types of provision allied to new patterns of immigration and inter-group power relations (Sachdev and Bouris, 1985). In particular, the increase of migrants from Europe into the urban areas of England has posed a challenge for and had a direct impact on the way in which Early Years settings tailor their provision for these learners with EAL. Research has indicated that a more diverse workforce tends to have a better understanding and awareness of the needs of diverse groups of learners in comparison with the indigenous, homogeneous groups of the workforce (Lumby and Coleman, 2008), the idea being that educational leaders need to harness the skills, languages and cultural awareness which is so important for understanding and relating to diverse learner groups.

Other major challenges in meeting the needs of learners with EAL

The educational landscape has changed enormously, seeing changes in the workforce and the ever decreasing influence of local authorities on settings and developing existing and new partnerships with other agencies in the name of multi-agency working. These complex ideas have required even greater leadership and management skills to ensure that whatever forms of partnerships exist, they have a direct impact on learners in Early

Years settings. Additionally, we believe that the aim of such changes was to improve the quality and training of different practitioners working in different settings for learners with EAL. The challenges have been legion, requiring fleetness of foot in leading and managing diverse staff and learners (Lumby *et al.*, 2005). Raising educational standards to improve diverse learners' outcomes is a major challenge (Reyes *et al.*, 1999; Bell and Stevenson, 2006; Heystek and van Louw, 2010).

Policy context

There have been many educational reforms, policies, initiatives and acts to improve the quality of education and care in England over the past decade. These have included the implementation of the Every Child Matters agenda (DfE, 2009), now disbanded, and specific to the Early Years was the Children's Act of 2004 (DfE, 2009). September 2008 saw the introduction of a national framework, the Early Years Foundation Stage (EYFS), in an attempt to bring together all aspects of Early Years from birth to age five, and September 2012 saw the review of the EYFS, with a change that separates the areas of learning into Prime and Specific areas to build on early development.

The Children's Act 2004 is a legal document on which the reform of learners' services has been based. The thrust of the Act has been to improve and integrate learners' services, to promote early intervention, provide strong leadership, and bring together different professionals in multi-disciplinary teams in order achieve positive outcomes for learners and young people and their families (Surrey County Council, 2014). The Act has aimed to improve effective local working to safeguard and promote learners' well-being, but there is in it very little detail of what such improvement for families of EAL learners will look like in order to shape their lives. The general trends and highlights of the policy context for learners with EAL are discussed next.

How the policy context impacts learners with EAL in Early Years

The aim of this Act is to ensure that EAL learners' needs are identified early to allow timely and appropriate intervention before such needs become more acute. But there are many questions as to how strategies will work together to better support families of EAL learners. There is an issue about the shortage of practitioners from minority ethnic backgrounds in particular, especially in rural areas, as well as there not being enough trained practitioners within the multi-disciplinary teams with bilingual and bicultural skills. What appears to be a major challenge for leaders in Early Years settings is how different agencies can work collaboratively to support the needs of learners with EAL. Better sharing of information is suggested in the Act, perhaps facilitated through stronger partnerships between settings and parents, as hinted earlier. Effective communication strategies then become imperative. We briefly review what Ofsted says about inspecting Early Years settings before we look at its suggestions about how to narrow the possible gaps for learners with EAL.

What does Ofsted look for during Early Years inspections?

Office for Standards in Education (Ofsted) inspectors are required to conduct Early Years inspections of different settings which have been registered on the Early Years Register

(Ofsted, 2014). Inspectors are required to gather the evidence they need from discussions and joint observations from the practitioners. We remain doubtful whether there are enough inspectors with expertise in EAL provision to make sound judgements on learning, attainment and progression, emotional well-being, and understanding of specific cultural needs, given the limited time they have visiting different settings in the country. In judging the progress of learners in Early Years settings, the inspectors are required to use the evidence to evaluate how well the practitioners know about, and understand, the progress learners are making towards the early learning goals. The inspector must judge whether practitioners have appropriately high expectations for learners. Our analysis of the Ofsted report (2014) suggests that many settings appear to face huge challenges to bring together and make sense of the varied evidence of Ofsted visits, parental discussion and the reflections of daily learning in the classroom. Detailed data analysis and subsequent action planning takes time, and this needs to be done when they are already facing mounting pressures to prioritise learning.

For example, the Ofsted report (2014: section 25:11) notes 'observations enable inspectors to evaluate the quality of teaching and care practices. They can judge the contribution practitioners make to children's learning and progress, and safety and well-being, especially the quality of adults' interactions with children of different ages'. There is no direct statement in the guidance saying how this may need to be thought through for learners with EAL. However, when tracking learners, the guidance does explicitly say that the sample should have at least 'a child from a minority ethnic group and a child who speaks English as an additional language' (Ofsted, 2014, section 30: 12). The following section delves deeply into the nature of attainment of learners with EAL.

Attainment of learners with EAL in Early Years

Attainment of all learners in any setting is a key educational task. There are different types of tools available to record progress and attainment of learners with EAL in Early Years setting. Equally, there are many differences one can discern from the range of schools and how they reflect the demography of their setting's context, that is, where do their learners come from, what is their cultural background, etc.? We begin by looking at Sylva et al.'s (2007) analysis of the Effective Provision of Pre-school Education (EPPE) data which reported that the great majority of differences in attainment between minority ethnic groups results from their demographic or background characteristics, with relatively little variation being due to specific minority ethnic group factors. For example, they noted:

- At age five, the Indian and Bangladeshi groups achieve better than expected scores for literacy and numeracy.
- At age ten, the Indian group continues to attain better than expected, while the Bangladeshi learners are now attaining lower than expected. The researchers conclude that the latter group does not benefit from primary education as much as other minority ethnic groups do.
- At age five, both the Black Caribbean and the Black African children on average attain higher literacy scores than expected, but do worse than expected for numeracy.

- By age ten, both Black Caribbean and Black African groups are doing worse than expected for literacy, but the Black Caribbean group shows slightly better than expected attainment for numeracy.

While the attainment of minority ethnic groups in settings is somewhat mixed, it appears that most of them catch up towards the end of primary education. The inspection framework (Ofsted, 2010) in England makes judgements on attainment and the quality of learners' learning and their progress by looking at outcomes for individuals and groups of pupils, and the evidence in the inspection process takes account of any important variations between groups of learners, and an analysis of the progress of minority ethnic groups which constitute learners who have EAL. Findings from section 5 inspection reports (Ofsted, 2010) suggest that the context of each setting is crucial in making informed judgements on raising standards.

Sims (2010) offers interesting challenges for all practitioners to consider for learners with EAL through analysing the statistics on the attainment of learners with 'first language other than English' (Sims, 2010). Table 0.1 shows that learners with EAL in Key Stage One (KS1) attain far less than English as first language groups. As learners with EAL progress up the educational ladder, their attainment becomes worse further up the Key Stages, which is in contrast to the EPPE data presented by Sylva *et al.* (2007). The data shows how imperative it is to continue to improve the attainment of learners with EAL as the inspection framework (Ofsted, 2009) has as its remit to inspect and make judgement of settings based on outcomes for individuals and groups of learners. This now includes evaluating provision and outcomes for learners of EAL (Ofsted, 2012). So let us discuss next what the Ofsted documentation (2012) means for learners with EAL in Early Years, given that the inspection in Early Years is contextually different.

What does the data mean for learners with EAL in Early Years?

According to Ofsted (2012: 3), EAL learners are not a homogeneous group, which means there are possible variations between individuals and even within minority groups

Table 0.1 Attainment of pupils with 'first language other than English' (after Simms, 2010)

	English first language	Other than English	Difference
Key Stage One APS[a]	15.4	14.4	-1.0
KS1 Reading APS	15.9	14.7	-1.2
KS1 Writing APS	14.5	13.6	-0.9
KS2 APS	28.0	26.9	-1.1
KS2 English APS	27.4	26.2	-1.2
GCSE 5+ A* to C	62%	51%	-11%
GCSE 5+ A* to C including English and mathematics	48%	34%	-14%
GCSE 5+ A* to C including functional English and mathematics	58%	38%	-20%

Note: [a]APS = average point score

within an Early Years setting. So practitioners reporting on the achievement of learners with EAL have to be mindful of individual 'linguistic, cultural and educational backgrounds' (p. 3), as these variations, according to Ofsted, are significant when interpreting the overall achievement of EAL learners. During inspections, Ofsted look for the teaching of literacy, including reading and mathematics. For example, within reading, Ofsted inspectors have to listen to learners, and 'discuss their reading with them' (p. 12), but they do not specify that this is only for EAL learners in Early Years. Excellence is judged through monitoring the attainment and progress of EAL learners who may be at the earliest stages of learning English (p. 3) and assessing the learners' proficiency and literacy in their first language (p. 4).

In making judgements about the quality of learners' learning and their progress, the inspection will also review analysis of progress carried out by the setting, including the progress made by different groups, particularly learners with special educational needs and/or disabilities; looked-after learners; particular minority ethnic groups, including Gypsy, Roma and Travellers of Irish heritage; those who join the setting other than at the normal date of admission; and those who are socially or economically disadvantaged (Sims, 2010).

Tracking attainment for learners with EAL in Early Years

In Early Years settings, it is evident that activities need to be matched to EAL learners' capabilities, which means that practitioners need to be aware of what their individual needs are within the setting. To see how a learner with EAL progresses and attains a high level, the practice often seen in Early Years is that of structured observations of the learner's behaviour (Mujis and Reynolds, 2011: 223). Another approach is the use of portfolios which contain a record of a learner's work at different times of the year, including the learner's drawings, practitioner's notes and photographs of the learner's work to evidence the Early Learning Goals (ELGs). The practitioners can then map the progress and attainment of the learner through dialogue, self-reflection and seeing what they can do differently from before.

The contentious issue of attainment for learners with EAL

One contentious issue of attainment noted by TDA/NALDIC (2009: 4) was the need for specialist EAL practitioners to have more focused training and advice on recording attainment. They also noted there was little evidence of team teaching or joint planning to support learners with EAL. This is confusing, given that the philosophy in Early Years settings is for a team approach based on focusing on the need to cater for the whole child. Some of the practitioners were not confident in their ability to use differentiation for learners with EAL and could not see the links between strategies used and EAL achievement in an Early Years setting. Notably, TDA/NALDIC (2009) found that identifying giftedness among bilingual learners was a challenge for practitioners. On another issue, TDA/NALDIC (2009) reported that newly qualified teachers found that EAL training on their courses was weak. This is now a focus of Standards for QTS, namely, Q5, which says 'Adapt teaching to respond to the strengths and needs of all pupils' (DfE, 2012b): Our analysis of some contemporary literature and Ofsted reports on the reporting of EAL learner attainment in Early Years found it to be rather sparse. For example, TDA/

NALDIC's (2009) report identified that there was weakness amongst some practitioners in the setting, not specified as Early Years though, and that assessment of EAL learners' needs was quite daunting with limited training and background expertise. Having considered some research that is relevant to identifying what the learners' and practitioners' needs have been, we now turn to consider how some of the above issues are likely to impinge on the provision for learners with EAL in Early Years.

Narrowing the attainment gap for learners with EAL in Early Years

In Early Years settings, narrowing the attainment gap is often achieved through encouraging setting-readiness skills. These may include the use of more or less structured play, small group or class discussion, paired or group work and circle time (Mujis and Reynolds, 2011: 227). We know from research that the home environment has a very strong influence on learners' development, and children of parents who actively promote learning in the home and are in regular contact with their setting demonstrate positive engagement with their peers, adults and learning (McWayne et al., 2004). Research by Hopkins (1994) suggests that to narrow the attainment gap, a setting needs to look at the following strategies:

- Targeting areas of learning
- Having criteria for evaluation
- Planning who will collect the data, when and what will be the source of information
- Having a systematic approach to the collection and recording of information.

This implies the need for strong systems of monitoring and evaluation of data to be in place, driven by strong leadership (Mistry and Sood, 2011).

Structure and organisation of the book

This book is divided into eight chapters. This introductory chapter outlines what we know about learners with EAL and how policy and context may influence provision for their learning. In Chapter 1, the term 'new arrivals' is explored and how to meet their needs is developed more fully. In Chapter 2, we look at working in partnership with parents of learners with EAL in Early Years. There we argue that the role of interpreters, community workers, language assistants, teaching assistants and others is crucial in fostering good channels of communication, and therefore strong leadership and good relations with the home/community become vital to help the learner flourish. In Chapter 3, we look at communication and language for learners with EAL in Early Years. We consider what practitioners need to think about in relation to learners who have EAL and the importance of regular interactions. In Chapter 4, we discuss the importance of assessment for learners with EAL in Early Years. We look at how approaches to the assessment of such learners are many and diverse, with different scales, procedures and types of evidence used by settings. In Chapter 5, planning for learners with EAL in Early Years is deconstructed. With the new EYFS, the importance of personalised learning is highlighted even more through the areas of learning. In Chapter 6, we will discuss the pedagogy of play for learners with EAL in Early Years. In Chapter 7, we look at using resources for learners with EAL in Early Years. There we argue that it is vital to use as many visual resources related to context as possible so that learners who have EAL can make links within the English language. In Chapter 8, we discuss how leaders/managers promote excellent learning environments for learners with EAL in Early Years.

Summary

In summary, research by Andrews (2009) and others has shown that all practitioners need to support EAL pedagogy and it is not the remit of EAL specialists alone. Learners with EAL are not a problem and settings need to continue to challenge such a deficit model. We need to remind ourselves that learners with EAL form a heterogeneous group. They include the newly arrived, those who are new to English and those who are more advanced bilingual learners but need further support with language use in academic contexts. So all will have specific needs that will require an entitlement to resources to enrich their pedagogical experiences to achieve attainment and success in education, whether they are in settings in rural or urban areas in England. There are therefore opportunities for collaborative working by all specialists and non-specialists. This offers additional challenges for school governors and requires creative thinking on how best to adapt organisational structure to address the ever changing policy context that will maximise the strengths of practitioners and allow them to best coordinate their EAL provision.

Our intention in this book is to ask the readers to reflect on these kinds of questions from their own practice in light of some theory and suggested practical strategies. There are no right or wrong approaches as each context is unique and this is the philosophy we wish to impart as each chapter unfolds. We are passionate about the quality of care and education provided for all learners and in particular those learners who have EAL; we are keen to learn more about how this practice can be shared amongst practitioners, leaders, parents and the integrated learners' services. This book is for all who care deeply about education and want to make a difference – especially for those learners who have EAL in Early Years – and we believe this includes practitioners, leaders, parents, carers, newly qualified teachers, higher education practitioners working with teacher trainees, support agencies and other stakeholders. We hope that this book is written in an informative and accessible way based on the link between theory, practice and critical reflection.

References

Andrews, R. (2009) *Review of research in English as an Additional Language (EAL)*. London: Institute of Education.

Bell, L. and Stevenson, H. (2006) Citizenship and social justice: developing education policy in multi-ethnic schools, in *Education policy: process, themes and impact*. Abingdon: Routledge.

Conteh, J. (2012) *Teaching bilingual and EAL learners in primary schools: transforming primary QTS*. London: Sage.

Department for Education (DfE) (2009) Every child matters, www.everychildmatters.org.uk (accessed March 2013).

Department for Education (DfE) (2012) *Teacher standards*. London: DfE.

Heystek, J. and van Louw, T. (2010) Leading in ethnically diverse schools, paper presented at the European Conference on Educational Research (ECER), Helsinki, Finland, Education and Cultural Change, 23–27 August.

Hopkins, D. (1994) *Evaluation for school development*. Milton Keynes: Open University Press.

Lumby, J. and Coleman, M. (2008) *Leadership and diversity: challenging theory and practice in education*. London: Sage.

Lumby, J., Harris, A., Morrison, M., Muijs, D., Sood, K., Glover, D., Wilson, M. with Briggs A. R. J. and Middlewood, D. (2005) *Leadership, development and diversity in the learning and skills sector.* London: LSDA.

McWayne, C., Hampton, V., Fantuzzo, J., Cohen, H. and Sekino, Y. (2004) A multivariate examination of parent involvement and the social and academic competencies of urban kindergarten children. *Psychology in the Schools,* 41(3): 363–77.

Mistry, M. and Sood, K. (2011) Raising standards for pupils who have English as an Additional Language (EAL) through monitoring and evaluation of provision in primary schools, www.tandfonline.com/loi/rett20 (accessed March 2014).

Mujis, D. and Reynolds, D. (2011) *Effective teaching: evidence and practice,* 3rd edn. London: Sage.

National Association of Language Development in the Curriculum (NALDIC) (2008) Languages in schools: more about the languages of bilingual pupils, www.naldic.org.uk/research-and-information/eal-statistics/lang (accessed May 2014).

Office for Standards in Education (Ofsted) (2009) *Twenty outstanding primary schools: excelling against the odds,* ref. 090170. HMSO.

Office for Standards in Education (Ofsted) (2010) *Inspecting equalities: guidance for section 5 inspectors,* ref. 090197, www.ofsted.gov.uk (accessed March 2010).

Office for Standards in Education (Ofsted) (2012) *English as an additional language: briefing for section 5 inspection,* ref. 090164, www.ofsted.gov,uk/resources/090164 (accessed May 2014).

Office for Standards in Education (Ofsted) (2014) *Conducting early years inspections: guidance for inspecting registered early years provision required to deliver the Early Years Foundation Stage, April 2014,* ref. 120087, www.ofsted.gov.uk/resources/120087 (accessed June 2014).

Reyes, P., Scribner, J. D. and Scribner, A. D. (1999) *Lessons from high performing Hispanic schools: creating learning communities.* New York: Teachers College Press.

Sachdev, I. and Bouris, R. Y. (1985) Social categorization and power differentials in group relations. *European Journal of Social Psychology,* 15: 415–34.

Sims, M. (2010) Narrowing the gap for minority ethnic pupils: recent findings from Ofsted, www.docstoc.com/docs/160036940/PowerPoint-Presentation—EMAS-4-Success-_Ethnic-Minority (accessed April 2014).

Stutman, M. (2013) Great quotes for kids about education and learning, http://inspiremykids.com/2013/great-quotes-and-stories-for-kids-about-the-value-of-learning-and-education/ (accessed May 2014).

Surrey County Council (2014) The Children Act 2004 – overview, www.surreycc.gov.uk/__data/assets/pdf_file/0003/168600/CYPP-Childrens-Act-Briefing-v2.pdf (accessed April 2014).

Sylva, K., Melhuish, E., Siraj-Blatchford, I. and Taggart, B. (2007) *Promoting equality in the early years.* Report to the Equalities Review. London: Cabinet Office.

Training and Development Agency (TDA)/National Association for Language Development in the Curriculum (NALDIC) (2009) The national audit of English as an Additional Language training and development provision, www.naldic.org.uk/research-and-information/ . . . /professional-development (accessed April 2013).

Chapter 1

Meeting the needs of new EAL arrivals in Early Years

'We must view young people not as empty bottles to be filled, but as candles to be lit.'

Robert H. Shaffer (2014)

The aims of this chapter

- To further develop knowledge and understanding of the term 'new arrival' for a learner with EAL
- To consider some of the needs of new EAL arrivals and potential challenges they may face
- To explore ways of supporting new EAL arrivals as they make the transition into the English educational system

Overview

This chapter begins with the clarification of the term 'new arrivals', which usually refers to learners who have arrived in England from abroad with very little or no English. They may include refugees and asylum seekers. Whatever their background, each learner and their family needs to feel as welcomed as possible by the setting embracing their culture, and this is considered next. Education in a new context and culture can be daunting for any learner, especially with the added complication of being taught a new language with different rules and expectations. The chapter then reflects on how this is achieved by ensuring that the learner has opportunities to play, interact, enjoy and socialise with their peers. The role of practitioners therefore is to continue to facilitate their learning to help them to increase their levels of confidence and self-esteem. Following on from this, the chapter focuses on a brief discussion of some of the barriers in meeting needs of new EAL arrivals. Finally, a global perspective in the curriculum is reflected upon to see what can be learned and applied in settings from a wider, plural perspective.

Key words: new arrival; EAL; parents; Early Years; globalisation

Introduction: who are new EAL arrivals?

The term EAL refers to learners who already speak another language or languages and are learning English in addition to this. However, the term bilingual describes a learner who uses English together with another language (DfE, 2007). Therefore a learner with

EAL can also be bilingual at the same time. But the suggestion here is that some learners with EAL may not have as much access to the English language outside the setting environment, especially if English is not the main language used within the home or with family and friends. In this chapter new EAL arrival encompasses international migration which includes asylum seekers and refugees, as well as national and local migration which could be as a result of moving home or school. Hence the term new EAL arrival is applied. Meeting the needs of global learners therefore imposes a number of challenges for settings in England.

For example, how to meet the varied linguistic needs of these learners with EAL? Also how can the setting reach out to the parents of these learners when practitioner shortage is so pressing? Or there may not be the socio-cultural awareness amongst the practitioners to forge links with these parents, who may be facing their own fears and anxieties regarding the English educational system and processes. These are just a few key challenges faced by settings that can probably be addressed through forging links with parents. As migrant workers have begun to settle and bring their families over to England, the demand for the support of learners with EAL has increased, as has the need for practitioners to develop a variety of teaching and learning strategies (Skinner, 2010). This chapter primarily focuses on meeting the needs of new learners who have EAL and who have arrived recently in an Early Years setting. We start this chapter by offering some background to new EAL arrivals.

Context of new EAL arrivals in Early Years

Newly arrived families at times may turn to others in their own communities to find out about housing, education and life in England, to translate and interpret, and to give them friendly, informal support. Many community organisations run supplementary settings to support learners' work as they settle in England so as to ensure that they do not forget their home languages and cultures (ContinYou, 2011). One example of this is home language classes at the weekend. Learners in newly arrived families, especially those seeking asylum, are at greater risk of changing home and setting several times within a short period of time. This can disrupt their education and make it hard to make sustained friendships. As supplementary settings receive learners from outside given catchment areas, they can remain a consistent resource for those learners who move regularly. In terms of an Early Years setting, each newly arrived learner with EAL has a right of access to the Early Years Foundation Stage (EYFS) (DfE, 2014). This therefore implies that this is the setting through which access to areas of learning should be encouraged in more creative ways that do not focus on language input all the time. This means that sometimes the main input could be through a video clip, or through puppets/pictures, or through play which helps new arrivals to observe and listen. The next section looks at some theory regarding the impact of the background of new EAL arrivals.

Background of new EAL arrivals

Vygotsky's (1986) socio-cultural theory understands human development as intrinsically social and that humans develop through lived experiences, social, historical and cultural. It is therefore essential to allow learners with EAL to develop their language and culture so that their lives achieve meaning through stories from their life histories (Holstein and Gubrium, 2000). It is through these stories that learners develop the language and culture they bring from home which helps to build their identities, which can be particularly visible through play.

Historical movement of people brought different cultures, languages and customs to England. We cannot just ignore them or ask learners with EAL to leave their culture and identity at the doorstep or at the setting boundary. As practitioners we need to embrace differences to ensure that every learner feels welcomed, safe, secure and happy, so that they will flourish in a caring environment. Research undertaken by Sood and Mistry (2011) presented arguments for the need to embed cultural values and beliefs in institutional practice which is paramount especially for new EAL arrivals. Their research findings suggested that practitioners wanted more awareness and training on different communities' cultural issues so that they were better prepared to meet the needs of such communities in order to better support their EAL learners in their setting. In this study, one Ethnic Minority Achievement Grant (EMAG) practitioner commented: 'We need more training in terms of how to access/plan for EAL learners specifically and also to have workshops regarding their culture for better understanding' (Sood and Mistry, 2011: 209). This is why a setting with a mix of practitioners from different cultures and backgrounds offers greater opportunities to mirror their setting's learner population. It is therefore important to see how the new EAL arrivals are made to feel settled, and this is explored in the next section.

Settling newly arrived EAL learners into the setting

An important task is to settle learners into an Early Years setting after an assessment of their linguistic skills, their background and their personal circumstances. The EYFS (DfE, 2012: 2) suggests that 'every child deserves the best possible start in life', hence some guidance on settling learners with EAL into a setting is important. Some examples of this can include home visits to aid familiarity of practitioner, parents and the learner, knowing the level of learner English language acquisition, being aware of prior learning experiences (such as being involved in toddler groups or play sessions at the setting), and encouraging conversations through play. This guidance could develop a better under-standing of the wider political, cultural, economic and ideological movements in the society from which the migrant learners come. This also helps practitioners to provide the highest quality learning experiences for learners in Early Years through promoting an inclusive culture (discussed later). Sometimes a learner with EAL may not have the opportunity or time to feel settled in the setting.

For example, Suzie was a Turkish female and, despite being born and bred in Eng-land, her parents made a conscious decision to keep the home language as Turkish as they did not want their daughter to forget her first language. When Suzie started school at four years old, she could speak no English. This meant that she was learning English as well as trying to access the curriculum simultaneously. Through observations, it was noted that Suzie copied other learners in the setting by following them and mimicking their actions, especially when it came to group activities set out on tables. But during play activities, she played alone and observed other learners as the setting had many toys that she had not come across before. One way Suzie could have been settled sooner into the setting was by being aware of some of this information in advance so that practitioners could create opportunities to support her language development through social interactions in play. Most settings do this very well and go some way in ensuring that the learner is made to feel welcomed and cared for as soon as s/he enters the setting. This means that all settings need to continue to be culturally and socially sensitive to learners with EAL so that these learners do not just become an invisible statistic in the setting. We have noted in the literature that having a cognisance of the culture that is inclusive for EAL learners, and others, helps settle learners, and its importance is considered in the following section.

The importance of an inclusive culture in Early Years

We believe that one of the key factors in settling learners is ensuring that a setting promotes an inclusive culture for learning. Every Early Years setting has its own unique culture made up of all the learners, practitioners, parents and the wider community. What is important to note is how inclusion is embedded in Early Years practice through the curriculum, pedagogy and ethos, particularly for learners with EAL. The importance of inclusion in the Early Years has been emphasised by the DfES (2007: 1, 2) it assists in:

- delivering improved outcomes for all learners,
- closing the achievement gap between disadvantaged learners and others,
- helping every learner reach their full potential, and
- ensuring that all families and their learners feel valued as part of the Early Years setting.

For learners with EAL this means acknowledging what they can do rather than what they cannot. This then helps to send a clear message to the practitioners and parents that the setting looks to strengthen the experience the learner comes with. An inclusive culture means, for example, talking positively about someone's customs related to a particular ceremony (such as a wedding or a christening), about the importance of eating certain types of food for a particular cultural group (such as the offering called prashad you get in some religious places of worship such as Hindu temples and Sikh gurdwaras), and understanding why this is important for that culture. Equally, an inclusive environment means correctly pronouncing a learner's name, regardless of its origin.

All settings try to be as inclusive as they can be and do their best to provide the highest quality education for all. They are also aware of the needs of learners with EAL within the context of an inclusive learning environment and culture. Our view is that inclusivity in Early Years settings will be demonstrated through certain qualities that we believe all practitioners need to embed within their practice, which are also key features promoted in the EYFS (DfE, 2014) (see Figure 1.1). The challenge is therefore to create a culture in the setting that supports and encourages practitioners in their aim to be inclusive. At the heart of Figure 1.1 are the concepts of tolerance and the celebration of difference, which is unique to every learner. We provide a number of examples in the next section to illustrate the central points of inclusive practice presented in Figure 1.1 to support practice in settings.

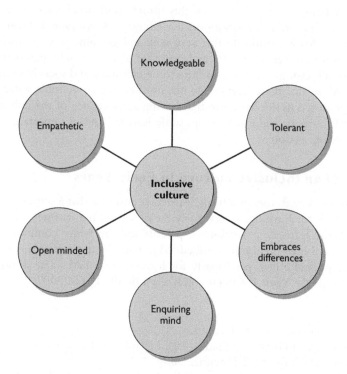

Figure 1.1 A mental map of features of an inclusive culture

Demonstrating inclusive practice

There are many ways in which inclusive practice can be demonstrated, but this is dependent on the context of the setting. India is a one-year-old mixed-heritage girl, and attends the local nursery setting three times a week. The practitioners at the setting made a huge effort to consult her parents regarding her specific cultural and linguistic needs to ensure that they were being as inclusive as they could. India's parents had no concerns as she was not talking yet and wanted her to be happy and mix with other learners in the setting as much as possible. The setting did not do anything special for her that they would not do for other learners. Their philosophy was to promote positive attitudes to difference from the very first day through making each learner feel special. This served to promote a culture of inclusion that the parents valued as their learners were happy in the setting. In addition the setting also felt they promoted inclusion through displays, key words, celebration of special events, the promotion of a listening culture, and the importance of involving parents as partners.

Promotion of positive attitudes to difference

We believe that promoting positive attitudes to differences, such as those of learners with EAL, is crucial in all Early Years settings as this engenders qualities of tolerance and empathy. By hearing different views and opinions, people can make inferences that will guide their behaviour. A negative attitude does not mean someone is intolerant or un-empathetic. It is when the behaviour and action resulting from such attitudes lead to stereotypes and discrimination that we need to address the situation. Through observation, debate and listening to each other we develop knowledge and understanding. As role models for our learners, we need to dispel any stereotypes about ethnicity and gender through using positive images of people and telling and re-telling their stories. It is equally important to field sensitive questions that may arise from the learners themselves sympathetically and in appropriate ways. One example to illustrate this was when a practitioner in a reception setting observed talk in the dressing-up area during free choice play. Neelam, an EAL learner, was asked by her peers 'Why have you put a scarf on your head? It's so hot today.' Neelam just shrugged her shoulders in response. The practitioner used this information to do a mini topic on clothes whereby she encouraged all learners to bring in photos of their family wearing special clothes to support discussions on differences in clothes worn.

Supporting the development of new EAL arrivals

The development of learners with EAL is more than just academic. The context of learning is vital as some learning experiences may be very different to what is expected, as shown by the next example. A reception setting focused on buildings in the local area as one of their topics. The practitioners took the learners out for a walk to look at different nearby buildings from the outside and inside if possible (Understanding the World; DfE, 2014). One such building was the local church. Parental permission was required, and the appropriate risk assessment had been carried out. However, some parents of newly arrived EAL learners refused to give permission for their learners to be part of this walk as they assumed that the focus of entering the church was for prayer and worship. In order to help support the development of learners with EAL, the practitioners met with each parent who had refused to give permission in order to explain the purpose of the walk (to look at different buildings and identify different features) and the expected outcome in more detail. Meanwhile the practitioners also began to gather resources for the walk such as cameras, sketchbooks, paints and crayons which aroused the interest of all learners.

The practitioners explained to the learners that they would also be required to draw pictures and take photographs, so the learners began to get excited at something new. The newly arrived EAL learners then told their parents that they wanted to go on the walk with the rest of their peers. To help promote positive relationships, the parents of these newly arrived EAL learners were also invited to be a part of this walk in order to understand what learning was taking place. These parents went on the walk and, for some, it was the first time they had entered a church to see the designs in the stained glass windows. This means that sensitively challenging the misconceptions of parents of newly arrived EAL learners and encouraging them to take part in setting activities builds stronger relationships and encourages understanding. This was a result of an accommodating setting team who celebrate differences, and therefore they made the effort in many ways to communicate with parents the purpose of the walk and its associated learning so that their learners were not excluded. This supported and extended the development of new EAL arrivals through the context of the topic, which also promoted the inclusive approach. We explore some of the misconceptions about new EAL arrivals next.

Challenging misconceptions about new EAL arrivals

Sood and Mistry (2011) found disturbing evidence of misconceptions and stereotypical attitudes about the ability of new EAL arrivals held by different groups of practitioners. A selection of these comments are presented next to show how some practitioners in Early Years felt about new EAL arrivals, especially when there was limited time and resources.

Comment 1: 'That these learners are not very bright' (practitioner comment from a nursery)

The context in relation to comment 1 is that, it is so hard when they first arrive at the setting, they have no idea of what to do or any understanding of what we are trying to say. It is also very difficult for us to match work to their ability as we have no idea, and trying to communicate is impossible. Therefore they are placed in the lowest ability groups for everything until they show progress. In this type of situation, one suggestion would be to carry out observations by different practitioners in the setting to gain information as to whether the grouping of the learner with EAL is appropriate after the first few weeks, especially if language is the only barrier. Sometimes, learners with EAL find the symbols in maths (such as plus and minus) much easier than words, and numbers in other languages (such as French and German) are the same as numbers written in English.

Comment 2: 'Lack of confidence from EAL children' (practitioner comment from a reception setting)

When we have new EAL arrivals in our setting, they always show the same characteristics in terms of being very shy, quiet and withdrawn. They will copy other learners especially when it is time to go out to play or going to the snack tables, but they will not select resources freely in the setting or go to a practitioner for help. If they are asked questions by the practitioners, they seem to freeze. In this type of situation, a suggestion would be for practitioners to intervene in play and ask general questions to all the learners, so that the learners with EAL have time to get used to hearing the questions before being put on the spot to answer them.

Comment 3: 'They may have Special Educational Needs (SEN)' (Early Years SENCO comment)

As many of our new EAL arrivals lack English language acquisition skills, we initially target them as having a special need until they have overcome the language barrier. However, whilst working on their communication and comprehension, sometimes additional needs are highlighted too, such as a lack of social skills in terms of mixing with other learners. In this type of situation, one suggestion would be to bear in mind that, with the opportunities provided in the setting, some of these needs such as a lack of social skills can be overcome with time. But it is also important to recognise the signs of other specific needs associated with development (such as autism/ADHD) with the help of the SENCO in order to best meet such learning needs.

These comments have huge implications for developing practice which needs to be inclusive and also to promote positive attitudes to difference. Migrant parents from certain parts of the world such as Europe cannot be assumed to have limited English, as some comments from interviews carried out by Mistry and Sood (2010) suggested that limited vocabulary of parents is somehow attributed to poor command of the English language for some learners with EAL. Indeed, there are many examples which show that new arrivals are highly educated and have high expectations of the English education system. So practitioners need to take time to get to know and understand their rich experiences, which can be difficult in a setting day. In the following section we consider how to meet the needs of new EAL arrivals.

Meeting the needs of new EAL arrivals

Murakami (2008) notes from her interview with one language support practitioner that 'everyone is just fumbling along' (p. 275) in meeting the needs of new EAL arrivals, which can be the case in white migrant rural areas where there are often only one or two isolated learners with EAL in the setting. It is important to highlight that this is an extreme case and perhaps gives us a good opportunity to research and reconceptualise what high quality learning experiences look like for learners with EAL in Early Years.

Sood and Mistry (2011) offered a number of examples of good practice, such as net-working based on focused topics and carrying out detailed information on EAL learners' educational backgrounds. Murakami (2008: 276) found that both teachers and support staff also wanted to know 'what to look out for' (e.g. like the silent period) so that 'we are more prepared for our new EAL arrivals'. This strongly suggests the need to forge links with parents and communities quickly. Teaching and learning resources should be written in clear and precise language and be easily available via the internet, for example, thus saving them time. Murakami (2008: 277) found that some parents thought work with new arrival EAL learners was an 'unnecessary distraction' and 'school leaders saw learners with EAL as learners having an adverse impact upon the school's public image'.

This shows how having the necessary knowledge and understanding of new arrivals' culture can help practitioners to dispel such misconceptions and stereotyping by working with the community through positive educational arguments. We consider this should happen whether one works in monolingual, monocultural, multicultural or multifaith Early Years settings. It is vital to remember that new arrivals add to the richness and diversity of the setting's ethos, culture and curriculum, and therefore it is important to recognise and value the positive contribution newly arrived EAL learners can make.

According to ContinYou (2011), the Department for Education (DfE, 2007) has identified four key areas of activity for mainstream settings with regard to new EAL arrivals. In Table 1.1 we have linked these to the four EYFS (2014) principles. Through our visits to many Early Years settings, we have highlighted what settings are doing to meet the needs of new EAL arrivals through the key areas of activity (DfE, 2007) to help support good practice. Each of the key area of activity shown in the table is explored next in relation to meeting the needs of EAL learners.

Table 1.1 Activities linked to the EYFS principles

Key areas of activity (DfE, 2007)	Link to EYFS (2014) principle
1 Providing a welcoming environment	Enabling environment
2 Supporting learners with EAL	Unique child
3 Establishing and maintaining an inclusive and welcoming ethos and curriculum across the whole setting	Learners learn and develop in different ways
4 Establishing and maintaining strong links with parents, carers and communities	Positive relationships

Providing a welcoming environment for learners with EAL

Fiona, the head of an infant setting, made sure she provided a welcoming environment by creating an entrance hall that is bright, airy and cheerful in presentation through the display of learners' work and the exclusion of clutter. Specifically for new EAL arrivals, there are welcome greetings in the different languages of the learner population in the setting, as well as photographs and artefacts showing special celebrations such as a Sikh wedding set in a gurdwara, a Hindu wedding set in a mandir and a civil wedding in a hotel. Fiona has ensured that all learners, parents, visitors and practitioners feel welcomed by providing such a stimulating learning environment including the outdoor area. In addition, she has ensured that a friendly and positive culture that celebrates differences exists. The practitioner experience in the setting has been positive in that parents have commented that they feel welcome and unthreatened when they come to the setting. This is supported by Dimmock (2000) who suggests that the physical learning environment needs to be conducive to learner's learning. Most settings are welcoming to their learners, parents and other stakeholders. They demonstrate this through different means of communication. But the first form of contact people have in a setting is normally with the reception practitioner(s).

Supporting learners with EAL

There are a number of ways that learners with EAL can be supported, especially when they are a new arrival. Sara is an Early Years practitioner in an urban infant setting and has some good ideas that could support practice. She has been at the setting for ten years and knows the local community very well, through making the time to converse with them. She also has the responsibility to support learners who have EAL, whether migrants or local, because she believes each learner is unique (EYFS). Sara's approach in supporting these learners is based on her own bicultural background and language ability used to communicate effectively with her learners in different languages. This shows how valuable a resource she is in the setting because she has formed relationships internally and externally where all feel comfortable in approaching her regardless of their level of spoken English. Sara has conducted many in-house cultural and language awareness sessions for practitioners to illustrate the principles behind understanding the uniqueness of each learner, but especially new EAL arrivals as their needs are contextually different. The parents look to Sara for assurance and she does that very well, ensuring she values their opinions and responds to their needs in an empathetic manner. This is supported by Miller and Cable (2011: 19) who argue that a shared multi-professional focus on the learner and family is critical for positive relationships. A diverse workforce of mixed gender and ethnicities is an ideal situation to have for a setting. But with diversity come the challenges of managing diversity sensitively (see Lumby *et al.*, 2005). This means that leadership and governors need to know the strengths of their practitioners to utilise their skills for the benefit of learners.

An inclusive and welcoming ethos for learners with EAL

Hina is an SEN co-ordinator in an urban infant setting. Her responsibility is to work with the senior leadership team and all practitioners to create and maintain an inclusive culture within the setting which has an 80 per cent EAL learner population. She suggests a number of ideas for supporting an inclusive and welcoming ethos, including: setting the vision (by discussing with all practitioners what makes the setting inclusive), direction and leadership for an inclusive culture (to support the translation of key ideas from leaders into practice); the learning environment offers challenge and support for all learners (to audit the indoor and outdoor environment to ensure that the resources used are inclusive as much as possible); sharing ideas of good practice with her team to secure success (by having regular team meetings), accountability and continuous improvement; working with and through others to design and shape flexible needs; and collecting and using data to gain a better understanding of learner needs and the local community to help inform how services should be organised (adapted from DfES, 2007: 5). By doing this, she is showing an understanding of the fact that learners learn and develop in different ways, and that the context of learning is vital. In Chapter 8 we discuss the importance of leadership in creating the vision for a setting. This means that it is not the headteacher alone who has to set the vision; it is a holistic activity requiring the commitment and buy-in of all practitioners and stakeholders. It is every individual's responsibility to ensure the maximum learning opportunity is provided to their learners and to be strategic in catering for the needs of specific groups in a setting.

Maintaining strong links with parents and communities of learners with EAL

Vimla is a bilingual practitioner in an Early Years setting with key responsibility for home-setting liaison. Vimla works through the setting's policy on home-setting links to ensure compliance with health and safety. She possesses great skills of empathy and cultural sensitivity gained through being a member of the local community. Therefore she has the necessary knowledge to know how to resolve issues and concerns of the community. Her linguistic ability helps to convey messages between setting and home with relative ease, which helps her to build positive relationships with parents early on. This is where all practitioners need to appreciate Vimla's cultural knowledge that supports her skills in decision-making for her learners with EAL, through understanding the holistic needs of the learner and being a role model and competent as an agent of change with the families she serves (Whalley, 2008). Our key message in this chapter and indeed this book is to ensure we foster good partnerships with parents. The school is part of the community and the community is part of the school. This symbiotic relationship glues the home setting together for the success of all our learners.

Strategies for supporting new EAL arrivals

Next we suggest some practical strategies for how settings support new EAL arrivals, based on a whole setting approach. These examples have been gathered through the authors' visits to Early Years settings and our own teaching experience. Many of the strategies below are examples of good practice, but are tailored to an EAL learner's perspective.

A whole setting approach to supporting new EAL arrivals

Early Years settings can support new EAL arrivals in many ways, but the key is to have a consistent whole setting approach so that all practitioners try to create the best possible opportunities. Ways in which this can happen include practitioners being aware of EAL learners' backgrounds as much as possible, and sharing information about cultural understanding and customs. All learners and their families need to feel welcomed, accepted, understood and valued if they are to engage in happy, successful learning, but more so if this is their learner's first experience of an educational setting in England. Parents' anxieties may be based on their need for greater information about the setting system, how well their learner will manage the transition and how their needs will be met. Therefore it is important that practitioners are able to ease these anxieties by ensuring that procedures are in place to support the learner, and if necessary the parents. In Table 1.2 are

Table 1.2 Practical strategies to support a smooth transition phase

Suggestions for:	For new EAL arrivals:
Aiding smooth transition	• Parents complete admissions form with support if applicable • Interview arranged with parents • Interpreter arranged if needed • Welcome pack and interview materials prepared in first language if necessary
Pre-admission interview	• Interview conducted by a member of the leadership team with practitioner (which should include reason for arrival or transfer from another school) • Family have a brief tour of the school and the new class • Learner/family information recorded on school documentation including previous schooling, health and dietary needs • Family provided with a welcome pack – translated booklet (if needed), home–school agreement and other information • Preferred lunch arrangements are discussed, e.g. for vegetarian pupils, those preferring to bring packed lunch, arrangements necessary to apply for free school meals • Parents informed of the possible start date
Period between interview and admission day	• Admission information given to school office staff to process and circulated to relevant members of staff • Prospectus and paperwork is explained to parents with aid of translator if necessary • School uniform is discussed with rules for jewellery, games and swimming kit, and naming items of clothing

some suggestions from experienced practitioners in the Early Years stage of primary settings to aid smooth transitions, firstly into the setting itself, and secondly from Early Years into Key Stage One, prior and post admission, which is also supported by the work of Mistry and Sood (2010).

While some newly arrived EAL learners will come from a different setting or country where little or no English is used, others may speak, read or write some English. Some learners born in England may have had limited exposure to English before starting school owing to their cultural background and the traditions of an extended family if applicable. Investing time in good admission practices is important for all learners, and especially for those who are new to the English education system. Some learners who come to England from another country can arrive mid-term. Successful admissions policies will enable them to settle quickly and begin learning so that experiences like that in Case study 1.1 are avoided.

Case study 1.1: EAL parents' perspective

Keya was born in England, but moved to Dubai with her family when she was two because of her father's job. Although her first language was Tamil, over time she became very fluent in all aspects of the Arabic language. After marriage, she came back to England with her husband and young child as her husband had a temporary job transfer. Although his competence and confidence with the English language was adequate, hers was minimal. After setting up home, both parents began making enquiries regarding a setting for their daughter Sarah. Both parents went to their local Early Years setting and made an appointment to see what their options regarding admission were. They were asked questions by the office practitioners in terms of address and reasons for setting transfer. Both parents then returned at a later date to meet the setting leader, whereby they were informed of the start date and the basic structure of the day. They were given documentation to take home and read, which was not explained, and no tour of the setting was given along with any explanation of routine.

When Keya took her daughter in on her first day, the setting practitioner showed where things such as coats and bags should go, but a comment was made regarding whether Sarah would be staying long at the setting if her father was only there on a temporary job. Keya became very anxious as she was not reassured or supported; the assumption appeared to be that they would not be in the locality long and therefore they were not worth the effort. Sarah stayed at the setting for a year before moving to a different Early Years setting. Ten years later, the family are still in England!

It is important to keep in mind that both learners and their families will be influenced by the messages they pick up about a setting from its environment and the way the practitioners behave. Therefore the early impressions of the setting gained by parents are important in developing relationships. Let us look at some of the practical ways in which a new EAL arrival can be settled on day one.

What to do on the first day with a new EAL arrival?

A learner with EAL enters the setting like any other learner with a reservoir of knowledge, understanding and experience. Our view is that a learner brings with them a fountain of knowledge, understanding and skills, and it is our role to help them make sense of this world (Understanding the World in the EYFS: DfE, 2014). We draw on Freire's (1970) humanistic ideology which suggests that when practitioners see themselves as partners with learners, there is a profound change in the practitioner–learner relationship. This process helps the practitioner to move from instruction-giving to a position of enabling; therefore the learner explores and creates their own meaning, which is a key feature of Early Years. This can provide a meaningful context which the practitioner can build upon. In failing to do this, practitioners are inadvertently giving out the message that whatever the learners have learned in life so far is irrelevant to their setting experience. Cummins (2000) argues that although practitioners are constrained to some degree by educational structures and policy, they do still have choices in the way they structure the interactions in their setting. For example, he notes that on developing the literacy of immigrant and minority language learners, the practitioners need to 'teach for cross-lingual transfer, and . . . do more to affirm students' identities in classroom interactions' (Cummins, 2012: 1973).

Induction is the term used to describe the period of the first few days when a new learner is settling in to their new school (DCSF, 2007: 40). Many settings have put in place systems to support this process, paying particular attention to the initial interview, initial assessment, providing a trained buddy or mentor, and tracking and monitoring to ensure that the new EAL arrival is settling and making progress as reflected in Table 1.3.

Table 1.3 is by no means comprehensive, but includes activities that settings have found useful when settling new EAL arrivals in and making them feel more secure in Early Years. In addition to going through such a checklist, it is important to look out for signs of stress, anxiety and aggression that may exhibit themselves in this unfamiliar context, and address these appropriately through the setting's policies and procedures. Assessment of each learner's need is a crucial first step as indicated above, so we need to ensure all practitioners supporting a learner are fully informed by assessments and monitoring how well the learner is settling in, and reporting any cause for celebration or concern. This can

Table 1.3 Practical strategies for settling new EAL arrivals in a setting

Key areas	Practical tips for new EAL arrivals on their first day
Admission form	Practitioners should have read the admission form for each learner in order to be aware of any confidential and sensitive information to support appropriate grouping
Friend/Buddy	Place learner with a friendly and helpful friend who can help them during indoor/outdoor activities, play and lunchtime, and also with classroom rules and routines
Language acquisition	Assess how well the learner functions in English and discuss this assessment and any concerns with the relevant practitioner
Parents/carers	Make contact with the learner's parent regarding any concerns that you need to discuss with them at an early opportunity: have parents had an opportunity to share their own concerns?
Health	Refer any health concerns to the linked setting medical team

be done with the lead practitioner or EAL co-ordinator to assess the learner's attainment and progress. The most important activity a setting is involved with is meeting and greeting the parents. We have to remember that this is an unnerving time for parents and it is our role to minimise their anxieties when seeing the setting as an unfamiliar site. The importance of looking at different learning approaches is developed next.

Learning opportunities for new arrivals

Learning opportunities should be planned to help EAL learners to develop their English language skills, and support should be provided to assist them in taking part in other activities. Some ideas that may be useful to support learning opportunities are:

- providing a range of opportunities to use their home language(s) through play, as well as hearing it through audio and visual materials, e.g. encouraging learners with EAL to bring in music that is common in their home, so that it can be shared with peers in the listening area;
- providing a range of opportunities for learners to engage in speaking and listening activities in English with peers and practitioners, e.g. using interactive stories on the interactive whiteboard which use repetitive language for learners with EAL;
- ensuring that all learners have opportunities to recognise and show respect for each learner's home language, e.g. in group discussions asking learners with EAL (maybe through the use of puppets as stimuli) how they say hello in their home language, and also valuing talk in different languages;
- providing bilingual support, in particular to extend vocabulary and support a learner's developing understanding, e.g. if possible using older siblings in the setting or parents or a translator to explain key terminology or new words to learners with EAL;
- providing a variety of writing in the learner's home languages as well as English, including books, notices and labels (if applicable), e.g. putting labels on resource containers that also include a picture for learners with EAL.

Next we explore the barriers encountered by new EAL arrivals.

Barriers to learning for new EAL arrivals

Practitioners need to continue creating an inclusive culture and ethos in their setting for all our learners. However, in a busy setting there are also a number of barriers that the authors have observed that hinder the progress of new EAL arrivals. It is important to identify what can be a barrier as it hinders learner progress, and therefore future attainment. If certain barriers are not addressed, then learners with EAL will not achieve their full potential, which in turn has an impact on standards at a later point in their education. What we need to avoid is learners with EAL just being overlooked. Some of the barriers observed are detailed below, together with examples of ways to address them.

- Lack of confidence in taking risks regarding different ways of learning for these learners. This means that planned activities may require greater differentiation more creatively to encourage greater enthusiasm from learners with EAL, which could be different to the normal ways of planning.

Example: having the confidence to try different strategies to aid comprehension such as use of pictures, puppets, video clips to help engage learners with EAL.

- Being worried that new EAL arrivals, especially mid-term arrivals, with little English language comprehension, may lower the attainment of the group in the setting as a whole.

Example: thinking of all learners as part of the setting family, rather than as a set of statistics that have to be achieved; it is about adding value rather than results alone. Maybe another suggestion is to keep a note of all the smaller achievements too, to help illustrate the value added rather than just the results gained.

- Lack of confidence in being creative through play, resulting in the silent phase in English language acquisition. This means that sometimes learners with EAL may just observe play or play alone silently whilst observing the language and actions of their peers.

Example: providing opportunities in play for learners to access unfamiliar resources, and allowing them to listen to the conversations of others in play. In this case, it is about allowing learners with EAL to take learning forward at their own pace in play.

- Lack of time in building relationships with parents who have limited understanding of an Early Years setting. This is about practitioners being too busy with other setting responsibilities to build longer-lasting relationships with parents.

Example: begin by encouraging learners in the setting to bring their parents in the morning so that they can do an activity together, or showing them something they have made. This means that practitioners can still do other jobs whilst also being visible to the parents as well as gaining information from observing the interaction between the parent and their learner.

It is important to remember that at times setting priorities can overtake the freedom to think creatively to meet the needs of new EAL arrivals. Sometimes support from outside agencies for specific language needs of new EAL arrivals can take time, and it is critical that learners are still integrated to the best of a practitioner's ability. In this respect, the vehicle of play both indoors and outdoors could be the most powerful tool to encourage skills such as collaboration, co-operation and conversations to support the initial settling in process for the learner.

We know there are a number of different means to address the ways in which learners learn. These may include approaches like active, reflective, pragmatic and theoretical learning (Kolb, 1984) or different ways of reflecting proposed by authors such as Moon (1999) and Wallace (2005). This means that practitioners can organise learning opportunities and experiences in response to learners' needs. Some of the frustration may lie in grasping how to provide a stimulating environment for different types of EAL learning needs with limited time and resources. An analytic approach may suit one learner but not another. With experience, practitioners will provide experiences to accommodate different needs. This has implications for organising the learning that exposes learners to various approaches, facilitates learning and supports young learners to work with peers who have different learning needs from their own.

Where new arrivals are supported in the setting by specialist practitioners rather than being withdrawn for separate sessions, Wardman (2012: 4) found this led to a more personalised approach because they used higher order thinking, questioning and feedback. It is these latter techniques that stretch the learners 'cognitively and linguistically' (p. 4) and lead to higher attainment. But we are uncertain whether adequate, focused training is offered to all practitioners in making this a reality for learners with EAL (Mistry and Sood, 2012). The challenge is to build in collaborative planning time with support practitioners that distinctly targets learning outcomes. The role of the setting is to educate the learner and we can do this more efficiently if we draw on the experiences of parents as partners in the education of learners. The practitioners need to continue to break down the barriers for some parents who for one reason or another do not like to visit a setting. An open-door policy in some settings helps, but each setting will have its own approaches to reach out to parents. Given the flux of migrants globally, this is an important topic to review next in the context of new EAL arrivals.

New EAL arrivals and globalisation

We introduce the word globalisation in this chapter because with a change in learner population due to migration patterns, we feel that such a perspective is important to deepen our understanding of our society and the English education system. Globalisation is about widening horizons of learners and practitioners. This may consist of learners' curiosity, widening learners' knowledge, understanding, skills and experiences to 'understanding the world' (DfE, 2014) from different perspectives (Mistry and Sood, 2012: 4). With such a globally rich tapestry of experiences, we have great opportunity to listen to different voices and study different policies that may help us to enhance learning to be more successful. However, we are in danger of being accused of not preparing learners for the wider world if we do not provide a broad and balanced curriculum. Good practice in Early Years is to extend the innovative learning opportunities to develop learners' thinking so that they become economically active citizens of the future. Examples of ways in which globalisation is being embedded in Early Years (Mistry and Sood, 2012) include:

- talking about special celebrations in circle time such as Diwali, Christmas and birthdays;
- discussion of human values through the prime area of Personal, Social and Emotional Development in the EYFS (DfE, 2014) that encourages greater cohesion, mutual tolerance and respect;
- bringing in the notion of culture through topic-based learning such as special day events to celebrate different cultures of the learners, such as an Eid day (Muslim festival), depending on the majority of the learner population;
- using topic-based, cross-curricular approaches such as world cooking where parents come in to help.

Global perspectives in education need to be embedded at the very beginning of a learner's setting experience and implemented in a culturally sensitive way. Genuine consultation will take time and effort, requiring diplomacy and tact.

A new vision of education is more focused on fostering learning in settings than was the case in the past. Dimmock (2000: 2) promotes a belief that settings of the future should be learner-centred, which is a key focus of Early Years, and argues for a development of a cross-cultural framework. This is where practitioners can develop a setting which embraces different cultural needs, a curriculum based on learner outcomes, learning process and experiences, practitioner approaches and computer technology. Here lies a challenge for senior leadership which offers great opportunity for free thinking to redesign their approaches. An additional challenge for settings is how best to nurture and support learners as flexible learners (O'Donoghue and Clarke, 2010: 6).

Summary

Whether learners are in families who are asylum seekers or those who have come to England in search of work and a better life, arriving in a new country can be a traumatic and overwhelming experience (Remsbery, 2003). Immigration to England has been happening for decades and settings in many inner-city areas have learned effective strategies to welcome and teach a diverse learner roll, especially at the very beginning in Early Years. We have considered a number of strategies suggested in the EYFS (2014) and from our own research that need to be in place to address gaps in learning for learners with EAL resulting from interrupted education. We have also suggested that practitioners need to use a range of teaching methods, supported by varied and differentiated learning materials and global resources that are appropriate to the different learning styles of the learners. New EAL arrivals need to be able to see themselves, their languages, culture and identity reflected not only in the immediate setting, but also in the wider setting and through an inclusive Early Years curriculum. Practitioners need to give the new learners space to grow confident and adjust to the English learning culture and also need to continue to be sensitive and diplomatic in working with parents/families to allow their learners to acclimatise within the learning environment. We need to embrace diversity and to celebrate difference by valuing each learner and the links made with their parents and community.

Reflective questions

1   What is the induction process for a new arrival EAL learner at a setting?
2   Reflect on how this process is different in Early Years in comparison with the rest of the setting (if Early Years is part of a primary setting)?
3   How are parents of new EAL arrival learners supported and reassured in the first few months?
4   How do practitioners in a setting continue to get to know parents of learners with EAL?
5   Try to find out through interacting with different groups of learners (both indoors and outdoors) how information on the needs of new EAL arrivals is being collected and used to support practice.
6   What features of a setting make it inclusive?

References

ContinYou (2011) How mainstream and supplementary schools can work together to support newly arrived communities, www.continyou.org.uk/what_we_do/supplementary_education/about_us/supporting_newly_arrived_communities/supporting_newly_arrived_c_1 (accessed April 2014).

Cummins, J. (2000) *Bilingual children's mother tongue: why is it important for education?*, www.iteachilearn.com/cummins/mother.htm (accessed March 2014).

Cummins, J. (2012) The intersection of cognitive and sociocultural factors in the development of reading comprehension among immigrant students. *Reading and Writing*, 25(8): 1973–990.

Department for Children, Schools and Families (DCSF) (2007) *Primary national strategy: New Arrivals Excellence Programme guidance.* Norwich: DCSF Publications.

Department for Education (DfE) (2007) *New Arrivals Excellence Programme guidance: a guide for primary and secondary schools.* London: DCSF.

Department for Education (DfE) (2012) *Statutory framework for the Early Years Foundation Stage (EYFS).* London: DFE, http://media.education.gov.uk/assets/files/pdf/e/eyfs%20statutory%20framework%20march%202012.pdf (accessed April 2014).

Department for Education (DfE) (2014) *Statutory framework for the Early Years Foundation Stage (EYFS).* London: DFE, www.gov.uk/government/uploads/system/uploads/attachment_data/file/299391/DFE-00337-2014.pdf (accessed April 2014).

Department for Education and Skills (DfES) (2007) *Early Years Foundation Stage (EYFS), effective practice: inclusive practice.* Nottingham: DfES Publications.

Dimmock, C. (2000) *Designing the learner-centred school: a cross cultural perspective.* London: Routledge.

Freire, P. (1970) *Pedagogy of the oppressed.* New York: Herder and Herder.

Holstein, J. A. and Gubrium, J. F. (2000) *The self we live by: narrative identity in a postmodern world.* New York: Oxford University Press.

Kolb, D. A. (1984) *Experiential learning: experience as the source of learning and development.* Englewood Cliffs, NJ: Prentice Hall.

Lumby, J., Harris, A., Morrison, M., Muijs, D., Sood, K., Glover, D., Wilson, M. with Briggs, A. R. J. and Middlewood, D. (2005) *Leadership development and diversity in the learning and skills sector.* London: LSDA.

Miller, L. and Cable, C. (2011) *Professionalization, leadership and management in the early years.* London: Sage.

Mistry, M. and Sood, K. (2010) English as an Additional Language: challenges and assumptions. *Management in Education*, 24(3): 1–4.

Mistry, M. and Sood, K. (2012) How are leaders integrating the ideology of globalisation in primary school contexts? *Education 3–13*, 41(5): 501–13.

Moon, J. (1999) *Reflection in learning and professional development.* London: Kogan Page.

Murakami, C. (2008) Everybody is just fumbling along: an investigation of views regarding EAL training and support provisions in a rural area. *Language and Education*, 22(4): 265–82.

O'Donoghue, T. and Clarke, S. (2010) *Leading learning: process, themes and issues in international contexts.* London: Routledge.

Remsbery, N. (2003) *The education of refugee children: policy and practice in the education of refugee and asylum seeker children in England.* London: National Children's Bureau.

Shaffer, R. H (2014) Inspirational teacher quotes, www.school-teacher-student-motivation-resources-courses.com/inspirationalteacherquotes.html (accessed May 2014).

Skinner, B. (2010) English as an Additional Language: an initial teacher education: views and experiences from Northern Ireland. *Journal of Education for Teaching*, 36(1): 75–90.

Sood, K. and Mistry, M. (2011) English as an Additional Language: is there a need to embed cultural values and beliefs in institutional practice? *Education 3–13*, 39(2): 203–15.

Vygotsky, L. S. (1986) *Thought and language.* Cambridge, MA: Massachusetts Institute of Technology.

Wardman, C. (2012) Interactions between EAL pupils, specialist teachers and TAs during withdrawal from the mainstream in UK primary schools. *Education 3–13*, 41(6): 1–17.

Wallace, S. (2005) *Teaching and supporting learning in further education*, 2nd edn. Exeter: Learning Matters.

Whalley, M. E. (2008) *Leading practice in Early Years setting.* Exeter: Learning Matters.

Chapter 2

Working in partnership with parents of learners with EAL in Early Years

'Children have never been very good at listening to their elders, but they have never failed to imitate them.'

James Baldwin (Edberg, 2014)

The aims of this chapter

- To be aware of some of the needs of parents with EAL learners regarding the context of learning in the Early Years
- To highlight the importance of working in partnership with parents who have learners with EAL in the early stages of education
- To be aware of some of the potential barriers caused by cultural differences in developing relationships with parents of learners with EAL

Overview

The key focus of this chapter is to gain an even better understanding of working in partnership with parents of learners who have EAL. We know from our own experience how daunting and complicated educational settings can be for many parents of all backgrounds, and therefore this chapter begins with a discussion of how the educational understanding of parents of learners with EAL can be contextually different and how it can be developed further through working in close partnerships with parents with advice from Ofsted. We then go on to explain how to familiarise the parents with the complexity of Early Years education which is contextually different to primary education through its focus on learning through play (DfE, 2014). This chapter also considers a number of approaches for involving parents in Early Years settings through case studies in order to help support practice. Next, there are suggestions on how to reduce potential barriers caused by cultural differences (some of which might be based on ethnicity), and finally we move on to how communication barriers can be addressed, especially where EAL has an overlying impact.

Key words: parents, partnership, home–setting links

Introduction

Parenting is a difficult and complex process as its practice varies within different cultures and contexts. But at the heart of all parenting is the importance of happiness and security for their learners in addition to the promotion of values such as 'resilience, well-being, self-worth, social competence and citizenship' suggested by Oats (2012: 1). It is evident from our experience that all parents, regardless of their background, beliefs and culture, want their learners to understand the value of working hard at a setting to become more successful in the future. One reason for this is that, for a small minority of families, the opportunity to have a good educational background may not have been a possibility when they were growing up, especially if they were migrants with EAL themselves; therefore this is an opportunity that is maximised for their learners. There are many explanations for a situation like this, but one reason for parents of learners with EAL wanting to secure the best educational experience for their learners could be to escape from the poverty trap and racism if this is the case. Modood (2005) points out that although Britain is far less racist now than in the past, there are still problems evident with what he terms cultural racism, which focuses on language, religion, family structures, dress and cuisine. Therefore, it is important to be aware that parents of learners with EAL can be just as much of a target for other parents at a setting boundary and setting events as can their learners.

But whether a family is from a highly educated background or not, they still hold the same high aspirations for their learner(s) to have the best education for future active citizenship. Therefore it is helpful for practitioners to know about the learner and their family's background, culture, language and customs, values and beliefs to ensure that transition into the setting is as smooth as possible. The role of outside agencies such as language interpreters, community workers, language assistants, parent assistants and others can help foster good channels of communication. We begin this chapter by trying to understand the context that can be associated with parents of EAL learners.

Why the needs of parents with EAL learners can be contextually different

All parents want the best for their own learners. This is no different for any minority ethnic communities or their learners with EAL. Their beliefs and values with regard to the education system in England need to be heard by practitioners in different settings to help better develop a common understanding for others' needs and aspirations. The needs of parents with EAL learners are distinct and can be different to those of the indigenous communities. This is because they may be more likely to meet prejudice, stereotypes and discrimination in more subtle and insidious ways (Troyna, 1993; Gaine, 2000). It is important to note that this can happen in both multicultural settings and so-called all-white areas, but it may just appear to be less visible in some settings in comparison with others.

We also need to bear in mind that in isolated areas, minority ethnic communities can appear to feel the fear of loneliness, isolation and oppression more than the majority population. In such circumstances, there are many ways to involve parents in local community events and the Early Years setting as suggested later. It is a fact of life that unfortunately some parents of learners with EAL may have experienced racism and as a result, they naturally feel the need to protect their learners from the devastating effects of racism, prejudice and discrimination. Little research has been conducted on the effects of racism on parenting practices or styles, but Garcia Coll and Patcher (2002: 45) say that 'on one hand, minority parents need to impart to their learners the philosophy that hard work and living a "good" life will result in rewards (i.e. meritocracy) . . . on the other hand, they need to prepare their learners for the facts that discrimination and prejudice may likely influence outcomes as well'.

Settings and the community need to work together to eradicate such pernicious effects on all, as discrimination and prejudice touch everyone. Cultural trust and partnership working is likely to make us all better parents in supporting our learners' learning, well-being and safety. Some parents may lack confidence with the English language and therefore they appear to be hesitant in contacting a setting to discuss matters concerning their learner. This is not helpful for either the setting or the family. Therefore many settings are doing great work in fostering such partnerships to encourage greater parental contact. Morning drop-in sessions, joining specific language sessions, and being involved in stay and play sessions with their learners in the setting are just a few projects that are run very successfully. We all know that developing and maintaining good relationships requires sensitivity, diplomacy and tact, and it is better to start from common, shared experiences which create a space for understanding to be developed even more deeply. This is discussed next through beginning partnerships with parents.

Beginning partnerships with parents

Effective partnerships with parents can begin through carrying out home visits if possible, which should not be restricted to just one visit prior to a learner entering the setting. A home visit to parents of learners who have EAL may appear strange and uncomfortable for religious, cultural or language issues, so it is best to be fully aware of the sensitivities involved. The Association of Teachers and Lecturers (ATL) (2003: 4) suggests the following benefits of carrying out a home visit by different practitioners (not just the lead practitioner) of a setting for building and maintaining strong partnerships with parents:

- an opportunity to establish early and positive contact;
- allows learners to be seen in their most familiar environment;
- an opportunity to meet other family members that you would not meet on a daily basis at the setting;
- a chance to see if the learner has any pets;
- appreciation of some of the cultural values of the home environment and understanding the impact this may have;
- understanding the roots behind any problems the learners may experience at the setting.

These points illustrate that it is important for practitioners to be aware of the different cultural aspects of parents of learners with EAL and the language(s) spoken to try to gain an understanding in order for effective communication to be undertaken with sensitivity and compassion. Working with parents effectively in Early Years is an integral part of the Early Years Foundation Stage (EYFS) (DfE, 2012: 2) which provides the framework for the provision of learning and development. The EYFS (DfE, 2012: 27) also makes clear what information settings are required to give parents, such as:

- how the EYFS is being delivered through themes and skills which are developmental;
- the range of indoor and outdoor activities and experiences provided;

- how learners with additional needs are catered for through personalised provision;
- procedures and policies of the setting to promote equal opportunities for all.

Ofsted (2011) suggests the importance of reaching out to parents of learners with different cultural backgrounds, including mention of Gypsy, Roma, Traveller, lesbian, gay, bisexual and transgender parents. The report suggested that there were different strategies deployed by settings, from specific role assignment, to unqualified practitioners, to shared roles with other settings or combined with other support roles (Ofsted, 2011: 23). According to Ofsted, whatever the role, it was generally highly valued by all. The issue is about having the right numbers of practitioners with the right level of skill, language and cultural understanding to reach out to different parents. We understand that some settings may not have the practitioners that reflect the culture of the setting or local community and yet have still found creative ways to resolve this. It may also be that practitioners need to consider alternative ways to meet parents, such as in community centres or neutral locations if parents feel threatened coming to a setting or practitioners feel uncomfortable about going into a particular family home. Thus, building up a repertoire of positive experiences and lasting connections is an important strategy that needs to be developed further. We consider two such examples next.

Example 1

In one setting, the bilingual practitioner was used to help deal with practical issues in settling a large cohort of Polish learners into a reception class in the setting. English classes for newly arrived EAL parents and their learners and orientation events were held to familiarise the parents with their locality. The setting also ran taster sessions in Polish language and culture, allowing the two cultures to mix successfully (Ofsted, 2011: 25).

Example 2

The headteacher at a primary setting used a part-time practitioner to work with learners who have EAL. This practitioner worked for two mornings per week on half-hourly sessions which took place outside the class group. Another example in the same setting involved a practitioner working with a group of three learners for twenty minutes three times a week to improve the learners' competence with speaking and listening. Such focused attention helped to identify individual learners' needs and what worked well for them. When the learners are not with the practitioner they are fully integrated in the class, thus minimising any time away from others (Teaching Times, 2012).

These examples show that Early Years settings continue to deploy their resources to maximise the learning opportunities for all learners. However, for learners with EAL, we note that the practical examples on how to do things with a learner will support them in making contextual and language connections.

The importance of working in partnerships with parents of learners with EAL

The central importance of relationships between the family and educational institutions for improving standards and attainment has been proposed over many decades. The value of holding regular parents' consultation meetings to discuss educational progress and issues is highlighted in section 33 of the Education Act, 2002 (Education Act, 2002). Such Acts have been influenced by international developments in social and educational research and, in particular, the interrelationships between policy developments and research. For example, the ten-year childcare strategy in England was published in December 2004 and set out the UK government's vision of childcare to 'ensure that every child gets the best start in life and to give parents more choice about how to balance work and family life' (Esmee Fairbairn Foundation cited in Daycare Trust, 2008). However, this strategy showed a low take-up of childcare among some minority ethnic communities for various reasons (The Ensuring Equality project cited in Daycare Trust, 2008), such as a lack of understanding as to the educational purpose of Early Years, or where other family responsibilities in the home get in the way. This means that in some situations some parents (particularly mothers) of learners with EAL from particular contexts may have other household responsibilities that come before participation in Early Years child care as illustrated in Case study 2.1. This has an impact on partnerships as there has to be a clear understanding of what the parents' understanding of Early Years education is and what the setting believes it is promoting through healthy dialogue and fostering open relationships.

Case study 2.1

Susheila is originally from Uganda and lives with her husband and mother- and father-in-law, and three children. She came to England after she got married, and has been here for ten years, with her youngest in the Early Years phase of the local primary setting. However, Susheila was well known in the local community for not getting involved in any Early Years activities that involved parents and their learners at the local setting. Susheila herself knows this, but finds it difficult to make the time to be involved and feels that other parents and setting practitioners do not understand her situation with her in-laws and household responsibilities. This is because she always seems tied up with household and family tasks, such as setting runs, looking after her in-laws, cleaning and constant cooking. Her husband works long hours and therefore does not have the time to support her with running the house. Susheila very rarely has time for herself, let alone time to engage with other parents or friends. This case study reminds us that it is important for practitioners to have some idea of the circumstances of some minority ethnic parents, so that they are not judged as not wanting to participate in their learner's setting life as a result of other responsibilities that take over. In this case study we noted why the need to understand the circumstances of some minority ethnic parents was important. The main reason was to ensure that empathy and common understandings about values and aspirations developed.

Practitioners in all settings are always striving to find new ways to keep minority ethnic parents particularly well informed of the developments in the curriculum and teaching and learning strategies. One example of this is where great emphasis is placed on the importance of maintaining the home language through encouraging parental participation through shared book sessions with their learner, including those parents who do not speak English. Another example is using parents of other EAL learners in the setting to support and mentor newer parents in the expectations and working of the Early Years setting. An additional example is where practitioners have focus parents' groups with a translator (if possible) to help alleviate any concerns about their learners in the setting. The importance of knowing and understanding some of the minority ethnic parents or family background is important to facilitate good relationships, and this is explored in the next section.

The importance of the home/family background

In both the Schools White Paper (DfE, 2010) and other literature, getting to know parents from different backgrounds and communities, and working alongside them in a setting, is seen as vital to enable the vision of partners together to be realised. Because parents of learners with EAL may have a contextually different home background in terms of language and culture, practitioners have to be creative in building partnerships (as discussed later). Early Years development (both cognitive and social) can depend on a learner's family background and parental behaviour. The quality of the home learning environment and parental aspirations are also found to be particularly important for learners' development as suggested by Johnson and Kossykh (2008). Learners' cognitive development is seen as an apprenticeship, meaning that 'it occurs through guided participation in social activity with companions who support and stretch learners' understanding of and skill in using the tools of culture', as suggested by Brooker and Woodhead (2010: 20).

The importance of cognitive abilities needs to be acknowledged as it demonstrates that even at an early age, differences in cognitive and social skills are not determined purely by nature, but, to a large extent, can be explained by differences in the family environment and parental behaviour (Johnson and Kossykh, 2008). If parents are actively involved in their learner's education in the Early Years, it will result in better outcomes especially in terms of 'cognitive development' (DCSF, 2008: 4), which in turn would also support learners' intellectual and social development. In addition, Johnson and Kossykh (2008: 6) suggest a number of factors that have a strong impact on learner outcomes in Early Years which link to the level of parental involvement:

1   family socio-economic status
2   parental education
3   home learning environment
4   quality of Early Years education.

We explore each of these four themes next.

Family socio-economic status

Johnson and Kossykh (2008) have identified in their report that socio-economic factors play an important part in the lives of minority ethnic learners in distinct ways. It appears that there are big differences between different ethnic groups. 'Learners from other ethnic groups make greater progress than white British children and achieve better than expected educational outcomes (except for Black Caribbean pupils, who under-achieve)' (Johnson and Kossykh, 2008: iv). Their research implies that parents from many minority ethnic groups particularly have very high aspirations for their learners and provide them with a good home learning environment regardless of their level of spoken English. But much more research and analysis of different variables needs to be undertaken to see how true this is for all groups of parents and learners. So we note that parental income, socio-economic status and parental education can make a difference in different societies. For example, learners from low-income families may be more likely to earn below-average wages when they grow up, compared with learners from more affluent families. This phenomenon is called 'intergenerational persistence' (Johnson and Kossykh, 2008: 1), which implies that our achievements in adulthood are closely linked to cognitive and social competencies developed in childhood and that development in Early Years depends on individuals' family background and parental behaviour. How true these observations are for specific minority groups is further discussed in Johnson and Kossykh (2008). An example to illustrate this can be found in Case study 2.2.

Case study 2.2

Vidya was from Fiji and a mother of four all under the age of eight. She came to England after her marriage with a limited understanding of English. Her husband worked very long and unsociable hours at an Indian restaurant. They all lived in a two-bedroomed flat, and could just about pay the bills. Therefore, it was very difficult to support her learners financially with any outings as a family, setting excursions or out-of-hours activities, or even resources such as laptops and ipads. Despite not having much disposable income, both parents had very high expecta-tions of their learners, and would do whatever they could to help with homework and additional reading. Over time as each learner overcame the language barrier, they would support the younger members of the family with all aspects of English language acquisition and setting's homework. These learners became very success-ful in their education and went on to become successful professionals, which they accredit to their parents' high expectations and personal sacrifice.

Vidya's case study shows that all parents want their learners to achieve the best they can regardless of their economic status. We need to be mindful that not all learners from lower-income families achieve less in comparison with learners from higher-income families, so need to be careful in making judgements. Most importantly, all learners need to be recognised as unique individuals in order to achieve their full potential. Next we consider how the educational background of a parent can influence their learner.

Parental education

From analysis of varied literature, the key message appears to show that over the years learners with better-educated parents start from a higher position and move to a still higher position in later years – whether this is through education or from a professional perspective. The opposite is true for learners of less-educated parents. The implication for practitioners is therefore quite profound when addressing the notion of equality. We need to create a learning environment that offers a level playing field for all learners. The EYFS (DfE, 2012: 7) suggests that in order to help create an equitable quality learning environment, you need a 'well qualified and skilled Early Years workforce which increases the potential of the setting to deliver the best possible outcomes' for learners, which in turn has implications for staff recruitment, retention, development and training against ever decreasing financial resources. The implications of this for learners with EAL are multiple. Firstly, where there are more diverse practitioners in a setting, their visibility and professionalism alone can have potential benefits for the learners with EAL as the practitioners can model effective educational support. Secondly, these diverse practitioners are a bank of resources with specific cultural and language skills that can benefit the learners with EAL and others. Thirdly, having a diverse practitioner team may help to attract other potential practitioners to come and work in a setting. Another example is demonstrated by Case study 2.3.

Case study 2.3

Chandar and his cousin were new EAL arrivals in a reception setting from a south Indian background. Both sets of parents had a basic understanding of English, but had no educational qualifications that were recognised in England. Chandar had just turned four and had a very limited understanding of the English language. On the other hand, his cousin Suraj who was five was fluent in English as he had already attended a private setting in south India that used English alongside the local language. One practitioner in the setting also came from a south Indian background and was therefore able to advise the other practitioners what was being said in Tamil by Chandar. This advice ensured that the learning was matched to both their differing abilities to ensure that they made progress. However, during free choice activities Suraj would still choose to go and play with his cousin and talk to him in both English and his home language of Tamil to help him make sense of what he had to do rather than seek the advice of a practitioner.

The case study shows that the skills of a diverse practitioner were highly valued in personalising learning for Chandar to ensure that he made progress. However, we are aware that not all settings will be fortunate enough to have this kind of support and therefore other suggestions would include the use of parents, siblings who are more fluent in English, or other family members who could help with communication initially. Regardless of the level of their personal education and qualifications, all parents want their learners to become successful. We also need to be mindful of the importance of the home environment in early educational development as discussed next.

Home learning environment

There is strong evidence indicating the importance of the early home learning environment (HLE), especially in relation to early educational development. Sylva *et al.* (2007)

show that, together with other family factors such as parents' education and socio-economic status, the HLE exerts an independent influence on educational attainment (at different ages). Researchers asked parents participating in the Effective Pre-School and Primary Education (EPPE) study (Sylva *et al.*, 2007) how often they engage with their learners in the activities that provide learning opportunities, such as playing with numbers, painting and drawing, being taught letters and numbers, and reading together, and combined this information into a single HLE indicator. The work by Sammons *et al.* (2002) found that parents who regularly engaged in playful learning with their learners did better on reading scores than learners whose parents did not do so. The implication for learners with EAL in Early Years is that some parents of learners with EAL may have little understanding about the structure, ideology and practice of Early Years in the English education system. So they may feel unsure and sometimes unskilled in helping their learners at home. This does not suggest that these parents were in any way inadequate in wanting the best education for their learner(s); on the contrary, many are very highly educated but are unfamiliar with the strategies necessary to support their learner(s), which is illustrated by the Case study 2.4.

Case study 2.4

Radha and Arjun were two five-year-old learners with EAL in a reception setting. Both were from a north Indian background, but not related in any way. Both sets of parents had high expectations for their learners to be successful and achieve to the best of their ability, but both were uncertain about how the English educational system operated in Early Years settings. Radha's parents were highly educated, and both worked long hours and therefore had little time to support her with any setting-based tasks such as sharing books in the home environment. Arjun's parents also worked, but he also had an aunty who lived with them, and therefore he spent a lot of his time with his aunty doing setting tasks, and generally engaging in conversations through play in the home environment. At set assessment points in the setting, Arjun's reading scores were much higher than Radha's, which was a direct result of having some support at home to reinforce the learning at the setting and to help make connections.

Case study 2.4 shows that parents also need to keep their learners motivated, active and interested through shared ideas as best they can, and practitioners need to continue to do everything possible to support parents' high expectations for their learners. Without this valuable support in the home environment, it is difficult for learners with EAL to make connections between the two environments to help them make educational progress. It also means more needs to be done to ensure that there is adequate home–setting liaison to share the concerns of each party. Let us next turn to what makes an effective Early Years education for learners with EAL.

Quality of Early Years education

There is compelling evidence showing that young learners with EAL benefit significantly from participating in good quality pre-school education (Sylva *et al.*, 2007). This is especially the case for pre-reading and early number concepts (Sammons *et al.*, 2002). However, despite this positive impact, there still appear to be fewer learners with EAL participating in formal pre-setting care. It appears that some mothers from minority ethnic groups are more likely to stay at home to look after their learners and to rely more on networks of extended family members, friends and neighbours. This may be an over-generalisation as the practice may be different amongst different minority ethnic populations (Aston *et al.*, 2007). Amongst traditional Pakistani and Bangladeshi women, their preference may be to stay at home to look after learners which lowers participation in pre-setting education, but also has implications for women's participation in the labour force. Case study 2.5 illustrates a challenge that can be faced by mothers from an ethnic minority background in relation to being torn between their responsibilities to their learner and to their family.

Case study 2.5

Ranjit was from a Punjabi background. She had two learners aged three and five at the local Early Years setting. When both her learners were at the setting part-time, Ranjit wanted to go back to work as a part-time florist. However, her husband and her in-laws did not share her view of going back to work as they were worried about what their community would say in terms of work being more important than family. Ranjit's eldest child was already full-time in the reception setting, so she increased the time her youngest was at the nursery setting, to ensure that she could work for 12 hours per week around her learners. Although her family were not happy with this initially, they soon began to realise that Ranjit's responsibilities to her family and the household were still carried out as normal. Ranjit made sure that she only worked when her learners were at the setting to ensure that her family members were not put to the trouble of looking after her learners or any additional household responsibilities. Over time the money she earned was also useful not only with household expenses but also to help support her learners with setting excursions and out-of-hours learning, which helped them to integrate more with other learners.

Case study 2.5 shows that it is a difficult task for the mother to juggle both family and her learners' needs. Maybe the whole family needs to understand the value and importance of Early Years education, as without these foundations, the impact on later outcomes for their learners may be affected. We now discuss why it is important to support parents of learners with EAL in providing high quality education in the Early Years.

Encouraging parental engagement

Parents as partners in their learners' education is a message constantly reiterated in this book. To engage parents with Early Years settings, a number of strategies seem to work well. Examples include services such as play buses, stay and play sessions and specific English lessons when the learner is cared for. Parents prefer having consistent practitioners who they can communicate with, trust and get to know over time in order for them to feel comfortable with the setting. The promised vision of a well-being service appears intact in the Schools White Paper (2010), but much of the detail seems rather sparse on strategy. Parental engagement in different educational settings appears to have a positive impact on learner outcomes. The National Association for Gifted Children (NAGC) (2007: 4) has suggested that parental engagement can be divided into five key areas (see Table 2.1). In addition, parental engagement has a threefold advantage: for the learners themselves, for the parents and finally for the setting itself (NAGC, 2007: 3). In the context of EAL learners, this can include better social, academic and developmental progress through aiming for 100 per cent attendance, which in turn leads to greater learner confidence and self-esteem, and hopefully over time fewer issues with behaviour at a later stage in life. For parents of EAL learners, this can include a better understanding of the Early Years curriculum and assessment (through communications to illustrate what learning is taking place at the setting, how and why), and how transition into Key Stage One and the National Curriculum can be made smoother. Finally, for the setting, examples include better support from the parents, which in turn may lead to an even better reputation for the setting in the local community.

Next, we identify some hidden challenges that can be associated with new EAL arrivals in the very early days of entering an Early Years setting and consider the importance of getting young learners into an environment in which English is used as the primary form of communication whilst they are still in relatively early stages of language development, but yet still supporting the use of the home language.

Hidden challenges and the importance of an English-speaking environment for EAL learners

Fumoto *et al.* (2007: 137) suggest the need to be more aware of and sensitive towards 'learners' ethnic and cultural backgrounds' so that settings can better create the social-emotional climate required to promote high quality learning and speaking of English. We have to be mindful of the fact that a new environment can seem to be a very frightening place for new EAL arrivals as everything from the routine to meeting the expectations of different practitioners and getting to grips with English very early on can seem confusing. Therefore the Dorset Early Years Team (2011) have devised a helpful checklist of how Early Years settings may be able to work with learners with EAL to develop greater confidence in speaking English. But we have to be sensitive in carefully handling situations brought about by some hidden challenges of cultural differences of EAL learners in the very early days. Here are a few examples that can help to support practice.

- Do not insist on speech too early as listening time is important for the learner to tune in to a new language.
- Some learners will not answer questions unless they know the answer, as an incorrect answer or a guess may mean losing face or being humiliated.
- Some learners may nod their heads to acknowledge a person but this does not necessarily mean that they understand them.
- Some learners will avoid eye contact with practitioners, as in some cultures this may be a mark of respect and does not indicate that they are not listening.

Table 2.1 Support that can be offered to parents of learners with EAL

Parental engagement from NAGC (2007)	Suggested examples in relation to learners with EAL in Early Years
Communication (examples that suggest how communication can be further developed between setting and home to engage parents in Early Years)	• Uniform (if necessary in reception classes in a primary setting) – maybe pictures of clothing to help initially, and addresses for where to get the uniform, through a display area • Start and end times of the setting day, through a visual timetable, including any special events taking place, such as a teddy bears picnic day • Being aware of the need for a change of clothes (for physical education or outdoor games) or footwear (such as indoor shoes and wellies) • Playtime and lunchtime arrangements – snacks, setting lunch/packed lunch/home lunch with associated menu and money arrangements
Pupil learning (examples that support parents in knowing what they can do to support their learner in Early Years)	• Key sounds and words – what they are for the week • Reading books – what days these are changed, where book bags should be kept • Knowing what the main theme of learning is for the week or term, and what parents can do to support it at home, through a leaflet or a notice on a parents' board
Parenting (examples that demonstrate the role of the parents in supporting their learner in Early Years)	• Offering parents translated key documents if required • Allocated time to allow parents the opportunity to talk to practitioners • Maybe a space somewhere in the setting, such as a parents' room, to allow parents to mix and communicate to support each other
Volunteering (examples of how parents can volunteer in Early Years to support their learner)	• Open mornings or shared sessions in setting to understand the routine and structure • Parents/learners shared reading sessions • Open play sessions whereby parents are involved in play with their learner to see how learning takes place in Early Years
Setting decision-making (examples of how parents can be involved in setting decisions)	• Reminder that outdoor learning is part of the Early Years curriculum so their learner will be expected to go out with the appropriate clothing • Discussion of home–school setting agreement if it has not already happened • Open door once a term to allow parents to voice their thoughts, concerns or needs in relation to their learner

Source: adapted from NAGC (2007).

There is also a strong suggestion that pre-setting start home visits to gain an appreciation of the learner's background can be of vital importance so that some of the above signs can be expected on arrival in the setting. Therefore it is important to have learners with EAL be comfortable in a mostly English-speaking environment as soon as possible. The reason for this is so that learners with EAL can become used to hearing certain sounds, words and phrases in different contexts through a relaxed play approach. If learners feel comfortable, then they are more likely to pick up key words. More importantly, by being in a mainly English-speaking environment, learners with EAL have greater opportunities to practise speaking and listening in English – which in turn helps their development in English language comprehension through appropriate contexts.

We have noticed in reflecting on theory and practice that the advantages of forming links with home and the community far outweigh the time and effort taken at the start to initiate change. This is worthwhile in the end as the learners feel valued and supported both at home and in a setting. Sometimes, it is important to remember that by putting the extra effort in with parents, they will help support practitioners in helping to raise their learners' educational outcomes. But there are many challenges, such as giving time to practitioners during timetabled sessions to set up meetings with parents, or there may be some cultural misunderstandings, and these are explored next.

The importance of the cultural aspects of learners with EAL

Being aware of and sensitive to the cultural aspects of learners is important, such as correctly spelling and pronouncing a learner's name and likes and dislikes as regards to religion and diets. For example, Sikh children often share a common surname such as Kaur or Singh, with Kaur identifying a female and Singh being ascribed to the male gender. Another example: as Muslims do not generally eat pork and Hindus do not generally eat beef, when snacks are prepared in early years settings, practitioners can make sure that learners' specific needs are acknowledged as younger learners may not be able to make informed choices and may just copy what their friends choose. So it is important to continue to engage with or inform the parents about the types of drinks and snacks that will be provided by the setting and to notify the setting if they appear to be unsuitable. As the learner progresses in settings, they become more independent and are more able to make their own food choices.

Another example of this includes the basics of pronouncing names of learners correctly as illustrated by Saieshwari who was a part-time bilingual assistant in an Early Years setting where practitioners and learners all call each other by their first names. Saieshwari has so many variations in the pronunciation of her name at the setting by different practitioners, that she just accepts what she is called as she feels it would be rude to correct other practitioners. It is important to note that there may always be a difference in the way different names from different cultures are pronounced. However, parents will appreciate the effort made by practitioners to get it as close to the real pronunciation as possible. It is important to remember that practitioners can sometimes spend more time with learners than anyone other than their parents, and therefore can be very highly valued and respected by parents, which is further discussed in the following section.

Potential partnership challenges

Some of the challenges in developing and maintaining good partnerships with parents and communities are associated with removing perceived and real barriers, like communication and cultural misunderstandings. Any such barriers can be overcome if people feel genuinely welcomed, respected and valued by listening to and learning from the learners and their parents and monitoring and evaluating a school's race equality policy.

To minimise barriers between home and setting, we need to explain to the parents how the learning environment in Early Years supports learners, both physically and mentally. Discussion with parents is therefore essential and Siraj-Blatchford (2010: 161) offers ideas for discussion such as:

- Family history – this could be in terms of where the learner's position is in the family (are they the oldest/youngest?), or whether any extended family live in the family home.
- Religious beliefs and practices – this could include important cultural events such as diwali and Holi (a spring festival).
- Learner's everyday life at home – are there any special home customs that practitioners would benefit from keeping in mind such as the food items eaten in the home that could be different to those mentioned in the setting (traditional foods such as flatbreads like parathas)?
- Language practices – being aware of the spoken languages in the home not only of the learners, but also of the parents.
- Parents' theories of learning – this could be a focus discussion point to ascertain what the parents view as good education, and then support this with learning examples in the setting.

The key message in the literature is that working with parents and local communities is essential to share cultural, linguistic and economic experiences. Alongside this is the report by DCSF (2009) which reinforces the value of a strong commitment to an ethos that promotes, amongst other things, high achievement, equal opportunities and partnership with parents and the wider community. It is important to recognise that in Early Years, learners come together for the first time from 'varied multicultural backgrounds that incorporate many different traditions and values' (Ang, 2010: 43).

From discussions with Early Years practitioners, Mistry and Sood (2010) noted the following challenges experienced by them in relation to building partnerships with parents:

- Not sure if parents understand what practitioners are saying;
- Worried about causing offence through words and tone;
- Lack of cultural understanding which causes practitioners frustration especially when parents cannot attend parents' events due to home cultural festivities;
- Frustrations when there has been minimal support from parents at setting events – which could be because they feel isolated in the community;
- Parents of EAL learners also not mixing with other parents and vice versa at events such as the class assembly.

In visiting various settings, the authors have observed that simple things often work best. For example, by regularly sending a one-page newsletter written in non-technical language (educational jargon free) sharing an idea or two about one key educational issue in depth. Another example is where we observed a short story input from a Sikh parent about their visit to the Golden Temple in Punjab to help with the topic of wonderful architecture (buildings). Such illustrations go some way in minimising the barriers between home and setting and in building good relationships to address stereotypes and misunderstandings culturally, socially or linguistically.

In mixed settings, where learners may come from different backgrounds, it is sometimes possible that we may misunderstand a learner's background and therefore we need to be vigilant in order not to inadvertently stereotype a learner or their parent as demonstrated by Case study 2.6.

Case study 2.6

When Sameer started at the Early Years setting, his mum was very keen to talk to the practitioner. However, the educational system in England was very different to that where Sameer's mum was born and raised – in Kenya. As a result of seeing a busy classroom with many adults, Sameer's mum withdrew and just communicated very simply in terms of basic greetings and a smile. She did not understand the busy reception classroom that seemed to have so many learners; more importantly she did not know how to express her thoughts to the practitioners. As the days went by, Sameer's mum became even more confused as to what her son did at the setting other than play.

Case study 2.6 shows the need to sit face to face with the parent to understand each other's needs and concerns. Time has to be invested to ensure that the parent feels valued and welcome to share any information. It is a partnership between the setting and the parent that must be worked on for the benefit of the learner. This is supported by Siraj-Blatchford (2010) who suggests that as practitioners we must ensure we do everything possible to help learners and their parents in the process of early socialisation so that it has a lasting impact on later life. This is likely to be more fruitful when done in partnership with parents, and is therefore investigated next through strategies to support practice.

Strategies for building positive parent partnerships in Early Years

Many parents of EAL learners have a rich cultural heritage that we can learn from. Cultural traditions can influence parenting through family structure, residency patterns, childrearing practices, and beliefs and attitudes about the roles of learners at different ages and stages (Garcia Coll and Patcher, 2002: 41). Acculturation is the process through which cultural adaptation and change occurs, so it might be useful to develop an understanding of this process in your settings. Below are some suggestions from experienced Early Years practitioners in settings to aid development of positive partnerships with parents, firstly in the setting itself, and secondly from Early Years into Key Stage One, which is also supported by the EYFS (DfE, 2014).

- Ask parents what they would like to know about their learner in the setting such as the learning that takes place, or the structure of the curriculum, or the importance of play.
- Look out for parents who hesitate in communicating with practitioners - they may want to ask you something but they may not have the confidence to do so.

- Be cautious of using educational jargon such as the Foundation Stage Profile that may cause confusion – parents would like to know how their learner is doing academically and socially.
- Have clear lines of communication including the use of interpreters if necessary that are evaluated over time – if they need immediate translation, check to see if there are any older learners in the setting who could help in the interim period.
- Be clear as to what the setting expects from parents at each stage over the year, so there is no misunderstanding – the idea is that by communicating with parents through translation if necessary, they are clear as to what each party can do to support the learning process, so that any additional needs are not overlooked.

Although it is common knowledge that the supportive attitudes, values and aspirations of parents can have a positive impact on a learner's education, the DCSF (2008: 2) suggests the following additional benefits of working with parents of EAL learners in Early Years:

- they are more likely than average to be involved in their learner's education;
- their learner is more likely to have greater improvements in reading, writing and numeracy;
- they will become more confident at helping their learner at home; and
- fathers also have a critical role to play in ensuring positive outcomes for their learners.

Additional strategies to overcome communication barriers

Involving parents from all kinds of backgrounds and ethnicities in their learners' education is common practice. What is more of a challenge is overcoming some of the barriers of communication between the home and setting. An example of miscommunication that may arise is when a message is sent home in a letter that may suggest one thing or another to the parent because it is written in an academic tone, thus making it inaccessible initially. So a better strategy is to send a short letter with succinct bullet points and leaving a contact phone number to get in touch with the setting if there are any communication difficulties. Another example of miscommunication may be to do with a misbehaviour incident by an EAL learner and the parent may feel anxious at the tone of the message calling for a meeting. Where possible, a phone call or a visit to the home can easily diffuse such tensions. Some additional suggestions of what can be done to support parents of EAL learners include:

- have some support workshops with translations if necessary to help parents understand the curriculum their learner will be following: e.g. an introduction meeting to the EYFS (DfE, 2014) curriculum with a translator present to describe the importance of learning through the role of play and creative activities that may be observed both indoor and outdoor;
- have a place in a setting where parents can chat to other parents informally without feeling under pressure – which would help parents get to know each other: e.g. maybe have a small parents' area (or a community room if space allows), so parents can integrate with one another for support;

- have a parents' resource library where parents can borrow resources to use to support their EAL learners such as games, books, puppets, DVDs, CDs, etc.; also make links with local community facilities that parents can access for support;
- emphasise the importance of the home language, and also show that its use is valued in the setting: e.g. welcome signs in different languages at setting entrance, and also valuing the use of the home language between learners and their parents;
- have strategy cards for parents for real-life learning that takes place in the home, such as reinforcing measurement through cooking, reading together in any language so that learners get used to books, the use of money in shopping: e.g. picture cards showing a sequence of events for cooking, picture pop-up books or sound books to engage conversations;
- evaluate the kind of support parents would like on a yearly basis, so that parents feel more involved: e.g. maybe by having a comment box sited near the setting's entrance to ask them how the setting can support the parents to support the setting and then having a system for evaluating parents' comments;
- provide practitioner training if necessary on effective communication with parents – maybe parents could be involved in part of this (in terms of good practice): e.g. visit settings with a higher proportion of learners with EAL to observe and share ideas of good practice regarding developing better communication with parents;
- encourage parent support groups in the setting: e.g. host a support group for parents and pair up different parents to begin a dialogue with each other.

Much of the extant literature is highly normative on certain aspects of parenting (e.g. high expectations and authoritative style from minority ethnic parents). But these are different in different ethnic and minority groups, so it is important to study parenting among specified minority ethnic groups to obtain an accurate picture. Garcia Coll and Patcher (2002), for instance, have found that there are some unique conditions under which minority ethnic parents have to operate. For example, a potential issue for such parents is the discontinuity between their cultural and social capital and that of mainstream culture and institutions. This social and class divide may not be so big within the majority culture. With the rise of migration of people from European countries, we have to be sensitive to other cultures, faiths, languages and customs, which can only enrich the setting ethos, if we continue to embrace difference and celebrate diversity in an inclusive manner.

Summary

The Early Years Foundation Stage (DfE, 2014) has made clear its aim of improving outcomes and reducing inequalities for young learners through an ethos of early identification and response to their needs which may, if not addressed effectively, lead to later learning difficulties, particularly in the case of learners of EAL. Therefore parents are crucial partners within the setting and in the education process of their learners. We need to do everything possible to understand and know about parents' needs culturally, linguistically and in other areas. Through effective communications and strong partnerships with parents, we are more likely to foster stronger feelings of being valued and supported to overcome any barriers between home and setting. Most importantly, good parental partnerships need to be embedded in the ethos and culture of the setting.

We have suggested that strong leadership qualities are necessary to ensure a holistic approach to communication with parents to reduce potential barriers caused by perceived cultural differences and identify how they can be minimised.

Reflective questions

- Reflect on the usefulness of strategies used by practitioners in a setting to ensure that names of learners with EAL are pronounced correctly.
- Critically reflect on what a setting can do to further support EAL parents settling into the locality or mixing with other parents.
- Try to find out through interacting with different parents what they feel are the challenges of supporting their learners effectively.
- What strategies can be observed in terms of reducing the barriers of communication between minority ethnic parents and the setting?

References

Ang, L. (2010) Critical perspectives in cultural diversity in early childhood: building an inclusive curriculum and provision. *Early Years: Journal of International Research and Development*, 30(1): 41–52.

Association of Teachers and Lecturers (ATL) (2003) *The Early Years: developing partnerships with parents.* London: ATL.

Aston, J., Hooker, H., Page, R. and Willison, R. (2007) *Pakistani and Bangladeshi women's attitudes to work and family.* Research Report 458. Sheffield: DWP.

Brooker, L. and Woodhead, M. (2010) *Early childhood in focus 6: Culture and Learning.* Buckingham: Open University Press.

Daycare Trust (2008) Childcare for black and minority ethnic families: summary paper, www.daycaretrust.org.uk (accessed July 2013).

Department for Children, Schools and Families (DCSF) (2008) *The impact of parental involvement in children's education.* Nottingham: DCSF.

Department for Children, Schools and Families (DCSF) (2009) *Building futures: believing in children – a focus on provision for black children in the Early Years Foundation Stage,* www.standards.dcsf.gov.uk (accessed July 2012).

Department for Education (DfE) (2010) *The importance of teaching – the Schools White Paper 2010,* www.education.gov.uk/publications/standard/publicationDetail/Page1/CM%207980 (accessed November 2012).

Department for Education (DfE) (2012) *Statutory framework for the Early Years Foundation Stage (EYFS).* London: DfE, http://media.education.gov.uk/assets/files/pdf/e/eyfs%20statutory%20framework%20march%202012.pdf (accessed December 2012).

Department for Education (DfE) (2014) *Statutory framework for the Early Years Foundation Stage (EYFS).* London: DfE, www.gov.uk/government/uploads/system/uploads/attachment_data/file/299391/DFE-00337-2014.pdf (accessed April 2014).

Dorset Early Years Team (2011) *English as an Additional Language,* www.dorsetforyou.com/355568 (accessed September 2012).

Edberg, H. (2014) 21 inspirational quotes on education, www.positivityblog.com/index.php/2007/04/20/21-inspirational-quotes-on-education/ (accessed May 2014).

Education Act (2002) Parent's meetings, www.legislation.gov.uk/ukpga/2011/21/contents/enacted (accessed September 2012).

Fumoto, H., Hargreaves, D. J. and Maxwell, S. (2007) Teachers' perceptions of their relationships with children who speak English as an additional language in early childhood settings. *Journal of Early Childhood Research*, 5(2): 135–53.

Gaine, C. (2000) Anti-racist education in 'white areas': the limits and possibilities of change. *Race, Ethnicity and Education*, 3(1): 65–81.

Garcia Coll, C. and Patcher, A. L. M. (2002) Ethnic and minority parenting, in Marc H. Bornstein (ed.), *Handbook of parenting*, 2nd edn, volume IV. London: Lawrence Erlbaum.

Johnson, P. and Kossykh, Y. (2008) *Early years, life chances and equality: a literature review*. Manchester: Equality and Human Rights Commission.

Mistry, M. and Sood, K. (2010) English as an Additional Language: challenges and assumptions. *Management in Education*, 24(3): 1–4.

Modood, T. (2005) *Multicultural politics: racism, ethnicity and Muslims in Britain*. Edinburgh: University of Edinburgh Press.

National Association for Gifted Children (NAGC) (2007). *The quality standards for parental engagement: a toolkit for schools*. Milton Keynes: National Association for Gifted Children.

Oats, J. (2012) *Early childhood in focus: supporting parents*. Milton Keynes: Open University Press.

Office for Standards in Education (Ofsted) (2011) *Schools and parents*. London: Ofsted, www.ofsted.gov.uk/resources/schools-and-parents (accessed September 2013).

Sammons, P., Sylva, K., Melhuish, E., Siraj-Blatchford, I., Taggart, B. and Elliot, K. (2002) *Measuring the impact of pre-school on children's cognitive progress over the pre-school period*. EPPE Technical Paper 8a. London: Institute of Education.

Siraj-Blatchford, I. (2010) Diversity, inclusion and learning in the Early Years, in G. Pugh and B. Duffy (eds), *Contemporary issues in the early years*, 5th edn. London: Sage.

Sylva, K., Melhuish, E., Siraj-Blatchford, I. and Taggart, B. (2007) *Promoting equality in the early years*. Report to the Equalities Review. London: Cabinet Office.

Teaching Times (2012) A helping hand for EAL pupils, www.teachingtimes.com/articles/helping-hand.htm (accessed September 2012).

Troyna, B. (1993) *Racism and education: research perspectives*. Buckingham: Open University Press.

Chapter 3

Communication and language for learners with EAL in Early Years

'If you talk to a learner in a language they understand, that goes to their head. If you talk to them in their language, then this goes to their heart.'

Adapted from Nelson Mandela (BrainyQuote, 2014)

The aims of this chapter

- To understand the context of language development for learners with EAL
- To raise awareness of some of the challenges learners with EAL may encounter regarding communication in the early stages of education
- To consider and analyse different practical strategies to support the language development of learners with EAL

Overview

Language is how we bond with each other, how we communicate and how we make friends, and it is the fabric around which we build our social networks. As more migrants from Eastern Europe are arriving in England, many settings are coping for the first time with learners from immigrant families who have little or no English. The DCSF states that settings should have a policy for 'community cohesion and engagement' (2007: 3), thereby making provision for their EAL learner population. This chapter begins with a brief discussion of the context of learners with EAL as this can be different to that of the homogenous learner population. Then it moves on to looking at how Early Years settings can provide more opportunities for learners whose first language is not English, firstly, through valuing the home language, and secondly, through language development including the role of Systematic Synthetic Phonics (SSP). Next we suggest some strategies that can be explored to support the EAL learner's skills in language development, especially if there is a cause for concern about language delay as suggested by the Department for Education (DfE) (2012: 6). The chapter then focuses on the impact of culture on language development, followed by possible challenges, with supported suggestions on developing good practice through practical strategies offered by Early Years practitioners.

Key words: language, communication, English, speaking, listening

Introduction

The National Association for Language Development in the Curriculum (NALDIC) argues that learners with EAL are in a 'unique and distinctive situation' in terms of their communication and language development (2006: 1). This suggests that some learners with EAL may not have access to the English language outside the setting environment and will therefore be endeavouring to learn it and access the Early Years Foundation Stage (EYFS) simultaneously. The Department for Children, Schools and Families (DCSF) highlights that a curriculum should be modified and redesigned where necessary so that learners with EAL can access their entitlement, including opportunities for practising English in context and with others, thereby increasing their speaking and listening skills (DCSF, 2007). We all live in a multicultural, multilingual and multifaith society, and therefore it is important to remember that all learners in a setting, including those who have EAL, have 'knowledge and experiences of languages and of varieties of the English language' beyond the setting which can be very different (Conteh, 2012: 22). Therefore, language learning takes place in every area of learning in education both indoors and outdoors, which encompasses a range of facets such as written, spoken, verbal and multimedia.

Context of learners with EAL

The Swann Report (1985) pointed out that learners with EAL were being taught in mainstream classrooms and were learning English simultaneously within the curriculum. Since this was reported in 1985, the main change has been increasing migration to England which has led to a greater number of different languages and cultures in our settings. Leung states that this policy was designed for the inclusion of learners with EAL and also to provide 'equality of access to education' (2007: 17). This suggests that in theory this will allow learners with EAL to progress on an equal level with their peers. However, the EYFS is developmentally structured, with the knowledge and skills of previous years being progressively built upon (DfE, 2012). This presents difficulties for EAL learners who are trying to assimilate the English language at the same time as accessing the curriculum, especially if they are new arrivals as well. Extensive research by Cummins (1984) established that bilingual learners and learners with EAL can take around two years to learn Basic Interpersonal Communication Skills (BICS). Table 3.1 shows examples of BICS with our examples to support practice for learners with EAL.

Learners with EAL in particular then require a further five years before becoming confident in Cognitive Academic Language Proficiency (CALP), needed in order to fully access the curriculum (cited in Conteh and Brock, 2006). Table 3.2 shows examples of CALP with supporting ideas for learners with EAL.

NALDIC (2002) suggests that BICS and CALP are an important area of consideration, with EAL learners being required to learn cultural and linguistic skills alongside academic knowledge, skills and understanding. One of the five outcomes delineated within the (now disbanded) Every Child Matters agenda is that all learners should be given opportunities for 'enjoying and achieving' throughout their school life (DfES, cited in Cheminais 2006: 22). This requires settings to develop the BICS and CALP skills required to provide equality of provision. In a busy setting the language needs of learners who have EAL can be overlooked 'because it is assumed that they will pick up English naturally and very quickly' (NALDIC, 2012). However, some strategies that could be used to avoid learners with EAL being overlooked include:

Table 3.1 How Basic Interpersonal Communication Skills (BICS) can be developed with learners who have EAL

Basic Interpersonal Communication Skills	Examples for learners with EAL in Early Years
Surface fluency	Ask very simple closed questions through play initially to assess depth of comprehension
Simple communication skills	Daily routine words such as playtime, snack time, lunchtime, home time
Relies on contextual support	Use of a visual timetable, or cards with key words and pictures
Face-to-face context-embedded situations	Use of face picture cards to show emotions associated with activities and instructions
Non-verbal support to secure understanding	Use of thumbs up and thumbs down, smiley faces, signing, gestures, using symbols to support understanding
Body language – gesture, instant feedback, cues and clues	Using stickers to show good responses, smiling, use of pointing and modelling

Table 3.2 How Cognitive Academic Language Proficiency (CALP) can help learners with EAL

Cognitive Academic Language Proficiency	Examples for learners with EAL in Early Years
Context-reduced academic situations	Allow out-of-context play and free choice
Needed for expressing higher order thinking skills (analysis, synthesis, evaluation)	Asking questions (what, where, when how, etc.), using photos for discussion though practitioner intervention
Language is dis-embedded from a meaningful supportive context	Collaboration with peers through play and games

- sharing her home language with the setting, and then using this as a common thread to share the languages of learners with EAL;
- making learners with EAL language feel special so that they have the confidence to communicate in any language through asking questions, and show and tell;
- using setting activities to celebrate the diversity of the learners so that being in the same class makes them feel special.

In these early stages of language development, the most effective means of helping learners with EAL to settle is to ensure that practitioners are listening to what they want, so that they help smooth the path from home (language used in this instance) to a setting. The assumption that learners with EAL have no language skills is incorrect. Learners with EAL do have language skills, just not in English in the same way as their home language, and therefore the learning context is of paramount importance. We cannot over-emphasise the fact that the language is part of any learner's identity and we should do everything possible to enhance and support this. Good practice shows that many practitioners are quite sensitive to the learner's home language as well as English. Crosse (2011: 15) says the priority is to ensure a safe and reassuring environment in which to learn and to encourage communication by the learner in as many ways as they can. Next we consider the importance of language in the Early Years.

Language in Early Years

All learners need language input that is clear, comprehensible and provides access to meaning, which is even more vital for learners with EAL owing to limited contextual experience. Much learning in Early Years settings continues to be practitioner-led initially and, therefore, exposes learners to much oral input over the course of a setting's day (Keum and Lewis, 2000). However, much of this input initially may not be particularly comprehensible to learners who have EAL, not only at the level of grammar and vocabulary, but also at the level of discourse (somewhat predictable and conventionalised ways of interacting in settings), and at the level of pragmatics – the way in which language is used to carry out specific speech acts such as to request or to apologise. In Early Years, written text in terms of mark making (initially), as a more permanent record of language development, must be seen as a major source and maybe a more desirable form of language input. Hence reading (or sharing books) must be regarded as a source of language learning as well as a skill in itself. For learners with EAL this places more emphasis on practitioners to carefully select reading material that will fulfil the criterion of being comprehensible and at the same time just beyond the learners' level of proficiency (Krashen, 1985) through more creative ways such as using role play.

Vygotsky (1962) suggests that all learners develop cognition and language through social interaction with more knowledgeable others. As more opportunities are made available by practitioners for greater interactions with EAL learners (such as through play in Early Years), they become more confident communicators. Initially, the practitioner guides the learners with EAL through relevant behaviour until they are able to perform the task independently and successfully. Through modelling positive behaviour and language, therefore, and familiarising the learner with the processes and procedures involved, the learner is more likely to become independent through new-found confidence. Next an example shows how practitioners can help learners with EAL assimilate and make sense of English language.

Helping learners with EAL to listen to and assimilate language sounds

Sarita is an Early Years practitioner from a Spanish background. She works in a rural setting where there has been an increasing number of new EAL arrivals from Bangladesh. Sarita allows time for her new arrivals to listen to and assimilate language sounds by allowing free choice play and also putting interactive sound games on the interactive whiteboard and tablets. She also uses arm movements and gestures to show her learners with EAL where things such as coats, indoor shoes and bags are kept. In the first few weeks she also takes her new arrivals to the various activities they are asked to do without the pressure of an end product before allowing them to choose. One of her strategies in the setting is to ask more confident peers to keep an eye on her new arrivals and to show them where things are if they get confused. She also tries to pair up her new arrivals, both with a speaker of the same language, if possible, and also with a more confident and fluent speaker of English. Sarita also uses phonics songs and challenges (with supporting puppets), songs to encourage repetitive words, the use of character masks to support role play, matching picture and sound/word cards, and lots of shared stories.

It is common knowledge that all learners bring with them to the setting a range of knowledge, skills, experience and language which serves as a springboard to the next steps of learning, including learners with EAL. As part of this process of scaffolding, practitioners need to make a link between the familiar and the new, and in the case of learners with EAL, a link between the home language and the language that is to be learnt. We know from theory that learning thrives in an environment where there is a balance of practitioner-led and learner-initiated activities (Crosse, 2011). Equally important for a learner with EAL is to have learning activities that will enable them to participate at different levels and 'contribute experiences from their own culture' (Crosse, 2011: 29). Currently, the English government's national priorities in education include early reading, which we focus on next.

Systematic Synthetic Phonics in Early Years

Currently there is a huge focus on Systematic Synthetic Phonics (SSP) in Early Years and primary education sectors by the English government and Ofsted (2011). Essentially 'phonics comprises the knowledge of the alphabetic code and the skills of blending (or coding) for reading and segmenting (or decoding) for spelling and writing' DfES (2007: 13). The Schools White Paper (DfE, 2010) identifies the importance of SSP as 'the proven way' to help learners with early reading (p. 22), which is a key skill as it helps in other areas of learning and enables access to the world. The Schools White Paper goes on to suggest issues with phonics teaching in the past and strives for a way forward to help resolve some learner's lower literacy abilities. This may be the case for learners with EAL, and therefore the Schools White Paper suggests that all practitioners have to 'ensure that all learners have the chance to follow an enriching curriculum by getting them reading early . . . That means supporting the teaching of systematic synthetic phonics . . . ' (DfE, 2010). For the practitioner this means that they have to provide as many opportunities for sound and words games as possible, with the support of ICT through the interactive whiteboard or tablets whereby learners can hear the sounds and mimic their formation. These key words can then be put in a play context to help contextualise their meaning. One way this can be done indirectly is through using more unusual role play areas (such as a space shuttle, or Noah's Ark, or under the sea) that inspire learners to use language for a range of purposes (DFES, 2007).

Case study 3.1

Mohini was an EAL girl in a reception setting from a South African background, whereby her first language was Afrikaans. She had a basic understanding of some English words to help with the daily setting routine such as snack time, outdoor learning time, choosing time, etc. Mohini had very supportive parents who spoke and understood English fluently, and therefore they would try to help Mohini with her spoken English. However, Mohini was very confused with aspects of SSP during setting activities. The reason for this was because her parents tried to help her in the way they were taught to read, write and spell, which was very different to the way SSP was being taught in the reception setting.

Case study 3.1 suggests that we should get to know the parents as well as their learner to share some of the ways in which aspects of the Early Years curriculum are taught in England. Practitioners employed as bilingual teaching assistants, bilingual nursery nurses and bilingual teachers may be called upon to act as interpreters in the first instance if necessary. The main focus has to be to help the learner and his/her family feel welcomed and at ease with their new environment so that interventions can take place if there are any signs of early language delay. Learning theories about language acquisition, language formation and development are not the key focus of this book. But we are concerned that if the language needs of learners with EAL are not understood and addressed by practitioners, then there may be delay in supporting their competence and confidence in language learning for socialisation. Therefore our next focus is on trying to recognise some early signs that could suggest a language delay.

Early signs of language delay

When working with learners with EAL in Early Years, practitioners may find it challenging to discover why they may not make progress in line with their peers, citing that either the learner is not grasping the English language or they have learning difficulties (Fumoto et al., 2007: 137). Hall (2001) reminds us that many learners with EAL experience a silent period when they are more focused on assimilating and understanding the English language rather than on spoken English. Burgoyne et al. (2009) found that some young learners with EAL had lower levels of English vocabulary and were not good at written and spoken text. Thus more emphasis on language skills is needed, like the simplified language materials critiqued by Rix (2006). Interestingly, we believe that making 'pedagogical connections' (Cadman, 2005: 353) rather than focusing on materials and teaching approaches might be a better option to encourage contextual learning for learners with EAL, especially in the Early Years.

According to Blackburn (2011), a delay in language development is common amongst learners with EAL initially, and therefore language learning skills through play are vital in Early Years as they have an impact on life skills in later years. Here are some examples from Early Years practitioners in terms of possible signs to look out for that could suggest a language delay for learners with EAL.

- Lack of interaction with peers, where learners are trying to speak through lip movement but the words do not seem to come out.
- Learners look confused when you ask them to complete simple tasks, and only understand what to do when copying their peers.
- The development steps in the EYFS for language and communication do not seem to be applicable for the learner.
- Learners do not show any interest in any aspect of SSP, and tend to make noises rather than form coherent words even in their own language.

It is important to be mindful that these could be temporary signs of language delay in learners with EAL, dependent on the context and learning opportunities provided, and therefore it is advisable to work with a setting's SEN co-ordinator if one is available. Other advice could be to seek the guidance of more experienced practitioners in the setting, or from another nearby setting in a similar context.

Allowing space for the learner to explore different learning as widely as possible within a safe environment is a hallmark of good practice. For learners with EAL, we can continue to provide rich experiences through stories, songs and poems, drawing, painting, using computers and engaging in other mark-making activities. Allowing them to feel comfortable and enjoy the setting environment will create opportunities for learners with EAL to open up gently. Below are some suggestions to encourage learners with EAL in Early Years to participate in collaboration and conversation with their peers and other practitioners.

- Allow learners to speak in their own language and dialect
- Allow learners to observe the setting and its routines
- Try not to correct them initially
- Possibly buddy the learner with another more confident learner for support
- Use of mobile play phones during role play
- Using interactive stories on the whiteboard
- Playing yes/no games
- Playing copy games

With a possible delay in language development it is important for all practitioners to remember that this can be temporary. It is essential that all practitioners in a setting provide as many opportunities for communication, language and literacy as possible (DfE, 2012) through structured and unstructured play. Sometimes learners with EAL just need more time to assimilate a new language and therefore could be going through a language barrier rather than a delay in language development. We consider whether there is any impact of culture on the development of communication and language ability in learners with EAL in the next section.

Impact of culture on communication and language

Hall notes that learners with EAL are often assessed as having a special need rather than as learners who are experiencing a 'temporary language barrier' (2001: 1). He goes on to argue that learners with EAL are making social and cultural adjustments as well as language ones, often causing them to be incorrectly labelled. This links to research by Gillborn and Gipps (1996) which led to them expressing concern that learners displaying language problems were often perceived to also have deep-seated learning difficulties. This is therefore one cultural implication for practitioners to consider when assessing learners with EAL (see Chapter 4). Another issue to consider is the understanding of different cultural attitudes, as explored in Case study 3.2. For example, in some Hindu families like those of the authors, an ability to read, write and speak Punjabi or Gujerati at home is considered an important skill. This ability is necessary in communicating with other family members (such as older extended family members) who may not speak, read or write English. So the acquisition of such languages offers a natural bond between the family members considered so necessary amongst Hindu families, and no doubt is similar in other communities facing similar communication dilemmas, often between generations.

The DfES states that in the twenty-first century cultural understanding is not an 'optional extra' (2002: 12) but an integral part of citizenship education, and Harries (2003) argues that through role play, learners with EAL in particular can explore the hidden curriculum, including cultural understanding and diversity, which is explored next.

The Bullock Report (1975) stressed that no learner should feel that they enter the setting having left their home culture outside the school gates. When considering the hidden curriculum of culture, it is necessary to examine the setting environment from an EAL learner's viewpoint. In order to feel secure and confident, learners with EAL need to feel accepted for who they are, regardless of ethnicity, faith or cultural background. This need for acceptance has been noted as 'crucial' (DfES, 2006: 7) if they are to successfully access the curriculum. Cummins suggests the importance of settings acknowledging a learner's cultural background, through positive inclusion and acceptance of cultural diversity, thereby allowing the learner to succeed (Cummins cited in DfES, 2006), which is illustrated by Case study 3.2. This case study shows that encouraging all learners to talk about their customs will help learners gain wider cultural knowledge which should be encouraged whenever possible through any context. The cultural upbringing of a learner will also influence the way they speak to people: some cultures refrain from making eye contact as a sign of respect, whilst others may treat this as insolence. Such cultural differences have been noted by the DfES (2003), which points out that learners need to be given time to adapt to the different ways of interacting with peers and practitioners within their setting environment before learning can take place.

Case study 3.2

The reception practitioner was looking at religious artefacts with her group. Sukhvinder, a Sikh boy, was fascinated with these artefacts. He was able to tell the class that his *papa* (dad) wore a *karpan/kirpan* (little ceremonial sword) under his clothes. The practitioner acknowledged these facts with Sukhvinder and encouraged him to say a bit more. But Sukhvinder did not say anything else as he did not have the knowledge and understanding to explain more about what he had seen. The practitioner acknowledged Sukhvinder's contribution and was able to show a picture of this *kirpan* in a book, then displaying it for the rest of the term. She was able to talk to the whole group about the use of ceremonial artefacts in different religions within the context of learners' abilities. Even the displays she had set up used the word *karpan/kirpan* to value the home language of the learner.

Both general language proficiency and literacy skills in a learner's first language(s) should be regarded as a key resource to support the learning of, and learning in, English. Therefore the use of a learner's first language is considered to facilitate language and conceptual development, especially in terms accessing and articulating content learning, therefore leading to improved outcomes for the individual. Below are some suggested ideas of how a home visit for learners with EAL can facilitate their language development.

• Firstly, carry out a home visit to see what level of communication can be observed between the learner and their family.
• During the home visit it may be worth doing some simple activities with the learner and their parent(s) or family to gain an idea of what their current level of language acquisition is.

- Begin a dialogue with the learner's parents to identify the home language(s) and to find out the key words used in the home setting. At the setting begin a key word assessment on a regular basis to assess whether the learner is picking up key words.

What these strategies suggest is that we should value the culture and first language of the learner and the family. The discussion with the parents is to ensure that practitioners promote a learner's holistic development first, which then leads to supporting additional language skills. Working with parents will ensure there is consistency of provision through a shared understanding of the individual learner's needs and security for the learners. Effective transition from home to setting thus becomes easier to manage. Language development of learners with EAL is analysed in the next section.

Ways to support language development

There are a number of ways to support language development in the Early Years. For example, first-hand experience and play form the corner stones of Early Years practice. Using different resources in different contexts will encourage learners with EAL to develop more confidence in speaking English. It is suggested that practitioners need to continue to offer support, guidance, encouragement and model questioning techniques in using the language in such situations. Table 3.3 looks at aspects of language development in Early Years with some examples to support practice.

The strategies outlined in Table 3.3 illustrate the need for practitioners to continue to offer their learners with EAL rich, deep and meaningful first-hand learning experiences that bring out their language competencies. As practitioners know, sufficient exposure to language could be brought about through creative learning opportunities like play or

Table 3.3 Practical suggestions to support language development in settings

Aspects of language development in the Early Years	Supporting examples for EAL learners in Early Years
Sufficient exposure to language input and linked opportunities to use language	Through contextual play with supporting key vocabulary, e.g. words associated with water play can include splash, pouring, swishing, floating and sinking
Opportunities for repetition in different contexts so that the expansion of language can take place	Key words such as snack time, play time, tidy-up time and home time
Model language conventions at any opportunity so that learners get used to hearing it	Develop this into a multi-sensory approach if necessary, such as feeling, smelling and tasting various foods with supporting vocabulary to get the whole experience
Give explicit language instructions on all conventions of language	Model how to say words correctly with expression and animation to make it more fun, including repetition from a contextual perspective
Set up contextual language boxes with items	Stories, toys, puppets, photos and books which are aimed at encouraging discussion linked to the class theme

seeing a puppet show and then talking about it through exploratory questioning. Next we consider some potential challenges faced by learners with EAL.

Potential challenges faced by learners with EAL

Learners need opportunities to use language in all areas of learning, indoors and outdoors and through play to which they have been exposed. For learners with EAL they need to do this through interactions that encourage them to test and refine their output under the communicative pressure of having to negotiate meaning. However, what seems to be lacking, particularly beyond Early Years settings, are opportunities to engage in inter-action with EAL learners. This is because:

- sometimes there are no direct translations for key words in certain languages,
- the same spellings in different cultures are pronounced differently which can result in very different meanings,
- sounds can also be pronounced differently in languages other than English, and
- isolated learning occurs in different areas of the EYFS, without language connections.

One of the biggest frustrations felt by learners with EAL is when practitioners do not understand what they are trying to communicate, especially when they are not feeling well or are hurt after an accident in the playground. Therefore, we develop next some possible strategies to address these challenges.

How have some of these challenges been addressed?

In Early Years, by constantly offering opportunities for different collaborative play, learn-ing contexts will enable learners with EAL to become more fluent in listening to and therefore using English. As practitioners, we need to continue encouraging all learners to express themselves in whatever ways possible so that they feel they are communicat-ing with us. We need to allow space and time for learners with EAL to make mistakes within a safe environment and to learn from them, especially if there are also issues with a learner's accent, as shown in Case study 3.3.

Case study 3.3

Amar was a four-year-old boy and a new EAL arrival from Belfast to a rural area in England. Prior to his arrival in England, he had only been in Belfast with his parents for a year, and had begun to attend the local nursery setting. Although his home language was Sindhi, both English and Sindhi were used simultaneously between him and his parents. Amar understood basic words in English and had been able to communicate with peers and practitioners through simple sentence communication at his previous setting in Belfast. However, Amar used to become very frustrated at times at his Early Years setting in England, not because he did not know the English words to communicate, but because his accent made it difficult for others to understand him.

Case study 3.3 illustrates that it is important to be mindful that issues with accents also need to be taken into consideration for learners with EAL. As practitioners in cases like this, we need to provide even more opportunities for learners to listen to language modelled correctly in as many different ways as possible. In addition we have suggested some ideas of good practice to help overcome some of the challenges faced by learners with EAL.

- Lots of use of gesturing, body language and signing to help learners understand basic instructions.
- Use of name cards with the photo of the learner to lend support with name writing and name recognition.
- Model play both indoors and outdoors so learners have an idea of a starting point in play.
- Use a visual timetable so that learners know what the routines and expectations are.
- Make several connections to the same word, and also use pictures to help if necessary.
- Use key vocabulary in as many different contexts as possible through videos, songs and rhyme to make it more interesting.
- Use of ICT to support verbal communication so that learners can be encouraged to listen and repeat independently or with support from a peer.

With any suggestion of good practice, it is important to remember that other factors such as the context and the learning environment are equally important. One reason for this is because language learning does not happen in isolation, and therefore to help learners with EAL make language connections, the context is vital in terms of repetition of key words and phrases to aid meaning. Let us look at some good examples of practice that promote language development of learners with EAL through an enabling environment by the practitioners.

Developing good practice: the environment

Learners' language and communication skills are acquired and actively shaped through the intervention of other practitioners as mediators between the learner and a social–cultural environment (Vygotsky, 1962; Bruner, 1983). Canagarajah (2004) suggest a linguistic safe house where learners can explore and experiment. Fumoto et al.'s (2007) study highlighted the importance of practitioners' verbal communication and sensitivity towards EAL learners' non-verbal expressions. In practice, we must continue to model practice based on our own ideology of teaching and the level of commitment to equity and justice linked to specific educational goals. The setting environment has to be rich in language learning which means the practitioners need to look at their own setting to see how it promotes inquisitive and questioning minds. For example, are there photographs about men and women addressing gender stereotypes such as fire fighters or police officers which may spark questions, dialogue and interest between the learner and practitioner? This implies that all learners, and especially those with EAL, have the experiences and opportunities for 'speaking and listening, and for sharing their ideas' (National Children's Bureau, 2010: 3).

These experiences in turn will help to promote early mark making, which then supports early literacy through the shapes of letters leading to the sounds of letters (DfES, 2007). The environment also needs to reflect the richness of literature, and therefore learners require access to a wide range of books in English as well as their home language. In some cases it is good practice to have story stations providing learners with the opportunity to listen to stories using ICT so that they can get used to hearing certain sounds.

In addition, there should be opportunities for the spontaneous use of language, especially through the use of role play. It is also vital to keep in mind that learning in the outdoor environment is just as important as the learning that takes place indoors. Sometimes, learning outside outweighs the learning inside especially when learners do not feel they are being observed or judged. This in turn helps to develop further the confidence and creativity of learners with EAL.

Developing good practice: the role of the practitioner

At the heart of developing good language and communication with learners who have EAL, or in fact any learner, is fostering good relationships with the learner, the practitioners and the parents. This implies the need for practitioners to continue to find different ways of communicating with parents and their learners, given that there are many more diverse communities within easy reach of settings. One of the less researched areas is how best to communicate effectively between practitioners and minority ethnic parents when there is not the same shared language. One key role of the practitioner is to model correct vocabulary and language through repetition in as many different areas of learning as possible so that learners have the opportunity to begin to make some links. However, this is dependent on knowing the current position of the learner both academically and socially. The EYFS (DfE, 2012) recognises the role of the practitioner through modelling, encouraging and supporting language. It suggests that young learners need to experience 'verbal and non-verbal communication' (NCB, 2010: 3). It also goes on to suggest that learners with EAL need to visualise practitioners using 'books and writing implements' (ibid.). This means that practitioners have to be seen to be speaking, reading and writing with young learners regardless of whether they can do it or not. Most important is the sharing of good practice ideas at the setting with the parents so that they can be reinforced at home, as shown by Case study 3.4.

Case study 3.4

Anita was an Early Years practitioner in a reception setting where 80 per cent of her group were learners with EAL, mainly from the Mirpur region of Pakistan. In her first few years of teaching, she had to make sure that she was visible to the parents both at the beginning and at the end of the setting day. She also had to invest time and effort in meeting and greeting all the parents of her learners, especially those with EAL who found it hard to communicate due to their lack of confidence with the English language. Anita began using strategies such as smiling to all, saying key words such as hello and goodbye. After days of saying similar words, parents began to respond to her by smiling and repeating 'hello', and waving goodbye. This may sound like a small achievement, but Anita was happy to find that parents were finally communicating with her regardless of their confidence with spoken English. Over time, the parents of her EAL learners would slowly begin to communicate with her through gestures and selected key words, to tell her if their learner was ill, or if they had forgotten their reading book. This was the beginning of building positive relationships with the parents in terms of communication, which could then support the learner in the link between home and setting.

Case study 3.4 shows that all parents want the best for their learners, and therefore they need to see all practitioners in the setting wanting the best for their learners too. When parents see practitioners sharing their viewpoint, they will begin to support the setting in different ways.

Summary

In summary, regular interactions through verbal and non-verbal gestures are key to supporting communication and language for learners with EAL. The development of language, certainly in the early stages of education, needs to be done on a regular basis: focused, little and often. The growth of a learner's confidence has a positive impact on their speaking and listening; it also adds to the rich cultural feel of the setting. This is not about dismissing an EAL learner's native language; rather it is about empowering them to be able more meaningfully to interact with life in English. Any language development opens up greater social accessibility. Communicating through simple key words helps learners to feel involved and less left out or confused. Learners with EAL should be made to feel that they can use their home language in the setting and that it is valued alongside the learning of English; therefore, to model such positive attitudes becomes very important for all those who work in the setting.

A number of theoretical and practical issues have been raised to further develop knowledge and understanding of how best to develop effective communication and language with learners of EAL and their parents. The related concept of scaffolding language development provides practitioners with guidance on understanding the important processes of learning for learners with EAL, and therefore enhancing their self-awareness and professional development through improving their everyday practice. Most importantly, communication and language in Early Years has to be taught in a fun and exciting way, so that learners become more enthusiastic as time goes by. Early Years settings can provide excellent opportunities through creativity and role play for learners whose home language is not English, which in turn helps to raise EAL learner attainment.

Reflective questions

- Reflect on the opportunities in a setting to observe English language being introduced to new EAL arrivals.
- Consider what strategies a setting can use to support the use of the home language for learners who have EAL.
- Indentify possible strategies that can be used to involve parents in this process.
- What kinds of activities have been observed in a setting that encourage collaborative conversations between learners who have EAL and learners who do not?

References

Blackburn, C. (2011) More than words can say: the diverse communication needs of young children in the foundation stage. National Association for Language Development in the Curriculum (NALDIC) Conference, Leeds, UK, 26 November 2011.

BrainyQuote (2014) Language quotes, www.brainyquote.com/quotes/keywords/language.html (accessed May 2014).

Bruner, J. S. (1983) *Child's talk*. New York: Norton.

Burgoyne, K., Kelly, J., Whitely, H. E. and Spooner, A. (2009) The comprehension skills of children learning English as an additional language. *British Journal of Educational Psychology*, 2009, 79(4): 735–47.

Cadman, K. (2005) Towards a 'pedagogy of connection' in critical research education: a REAL story. *Journal of English for Academic Purposes*, 4(4): 353–67.

Canagarajah, S. (2004) Subversive identities, pedagogical safe houses, and critical learning, in B. Norton and K. Toohey (eds), *Critical pedagogies and language learning*. Cambridge: Cambridge University Press, pp. 116–37.

Cheminais, R. (2006) *Every child matters: a practical guide for teachers*. London: David Fulton.

Conteh, J. (2012) *Teaching bilingual and EAL learners in primary schools*. London: Sage and Learning Matters, pp. 87–100.

Conteh, J. and Brock, A. (2006) Introduction: principles and practices for teaching bilingual learners, in J. Conteh (ed.), *Promoting learning for bilingual pupils 3–11: opening doors to success*. London: Paul Chapman.

Crosse, K. (2011) *Introducing English as an additional language to young children*. London: Sage.

Cummins, J. (1984) *Bilingual education and special education: issues in assessment and pedagogy*. San Diego: College Hill.

Department for Children, Schools and Families (DCSF) (2007) *Primary national strategy: supporting children learning English as an additional language: guidance for practitioners in the Early Years Foundation Stage*. Norwich: DCSF Publications.

Department for Education (DfE) (2010) *The importance of teaching: the Schools White Paper 2010*, https://www.education.gov.uk/publications/eOrderingDownload/CM-7980.pdf (accessed 3 January 2013).

Department for Education (DfE) (2012) *Statutory framework for the Early Years Foundation Stage (EYFS)*. London: DfE, http://media.education.gov.uk/assets/files/pdf/e/eyfs%20statutory%20framework%20 march%202012.pdf (accessed January 2013).

Department for Education and Skills (DfES) (1975) *The Bullock Report (A language for life)*, London: DfES.

Department for Education and Skills (DfES) (2002) *English as an Additional Language: induction training for teaching assistants in primary and secondary school*. London: DfES Publications.

Department for Education and Skills (DfES) (2003) *Speaking, listening and learning: working with children in Key Stages 1 and 2*. Norwich: DfES Publications.

Department for Education and Skills (DfES) (2006) *Excellence and enjoyment: learning and teaching for bilingual children in the primary years: Unit 3: Creating an inclusive learning culture*. Norwich: DfES Publications.

Department for Education and Skills (DFES) (2007) *Letters and sounds: principles and practise of high quality phonics*. London: Primary National Strategy, DfES.

Fumoto, H., Hargreaves, D. J. and Maxwell, S. (2007) Teachers' perceptions of their relationships with children who speak English as an additional language in early childhood settings. *Journal of Early Childhood Research*, 5(2): 135–53.

Gillborn, D. and Gipps, C. (1996) *Recent research in the achievements of ethnic minority pupils*. London: HMSO.

Hall, D. (2001) *Assessing the needs of bilingual pupils: living in two languages*. Revised by D. Griffiths, L. Haslam and Y. Wilkin. 2nd edn. London: David Fulton.

Harries, J. (2003) *Role play: the value of role play, managing role play, 18 scenarios with links to ELGs*. Leamington Spa: Step Forward Publishing.

Keum, J. and Lewis, M. (2000) Language demands in New Zealand secondary school classrooms. *Many Voices*, 15: 4–6.

Krashen, S. D. (1985) *The input hypothesis*. London: Longman.

Leung, C. (2007) English as an Additional Language policy: issues of inclusive access and language learning in the mainstream. *Naldic Quarterly* 4(3): 17–24.

National Association for Language Development in the Curriculum (NALDIC) (2002). *The EAL teacher: descriptors of good practice*. Watford: National Association for Language Development in the Curriculum.

National Association of Language Development in the Curriculum (NALDIC) (2006) *Response to the Rose review of the teaching of reading and the NLS*. Watford: National Association for Language Development in the Curriculum.

National Association for Language Development in the Curriculum (NALDIC) (2012) *EYFS and EAL: supporting bilingual children in the Early Years*, www.naldic.org.uk/eal-teaching-and-learning/outline-guidance/early-years (accessed November 2012).

National Children's Bureau (NCB) (2010) *Communication, language and literacy and the Early Years Foundation Stage*. London: NCB.

Office for Standards in Education (Ofsted) (2011) *Getting them reading early*. Manchester: Ofsted.

Rix, J. (2006) Simplified language materials: heir usage and value to teachers and support staff in mainstream settings. *Teaching and Teacher Education*, 22(8): 1145–56.

Swann, M. (1985) *Education for all: the report of the committee of inquiry into the education of children from ethnic minority groups*. London: HMSO.

Vygotsky, L. (1962) *Thought and language*. Cambridge, MA: MIT Press.

Wood, D., Bruner, J. and Ross, G. (1976) The role of tutoring in problem-solving. *Journal of Child Psychology and Psychiatry*, 17(2): 89–100.

Chapter 4

Assessment for learners with EAL in Early Years

'The "skills escalator" embodies an approach in which practitioners constantly renew and extend their skills and knowledge, enabling them to move up the escalator.'
Metaphor borrowed from the Department of Health (2007)

The aims of this chapter

- To develop knowledge and understanding of why assessment for learners with EAL may be different
- To be aware of some of the challenges in assessing learners with EAL
- To consider different practical strategies which support the assessment process for learners with EAL

Overview

Assessment is an important aspect of monitoring and evaluating how well all learners are making progress in any setting and, in particular, it is about tracking the progress of the unique learning journey of each individual. The assessment of learners in Early Years is often carried out differently from assessment in the rest of a setting owing to the contextual nature of this age phase and the different curriculum. This chapter begins by discussing why assessment tools need to be more personalised by practitioners for learners with EAL. One reason for this is because the needs of learners with EAL are different to those of indigenous learners in terms of their cultural, linguistic and developmental needs. Next, we look at different examples of assessment and how assessment of learners with EAL in Early Years can be tracked as a continuous process which starts at the first point of contact. The discussion then focuses on why the ongoing and continuous assessment of a learner's proficiency in English cannot be assessed through the Foundation Stage e-profile or Early Years Outcomes alone. We also argue that practitioners working with EAL learners will need to know at some depth the level of proficiency in the use of English they have in order to effectively assess, plan and monitor their progress in the curriculum. The chapter concludes by noting that without the variety of evidence gained through assessment via the use of some suggested templates, effective planning for effective learning by learners with EAL may prove to be challenging.

Key words: formative and summative assessment, e-profile, monitoring, evaluating

Introduction

It is essential to be clear on how Early Years provision, assessment of progress and the setting of targets for learners learning EAL relates to broader national initiatives, especially in relation to curriculum changes. The assessment of a learner's learning and development in Early Years has recently taken on greater importance in terms of developing guidance such as the Early Years Foundation Stage Profile (EYFSP) (DfE, 2013a). This increased priority is to help practitioners to better meet and track the needs of all, especially those learners from economically disadvantaged backgrounds and communities, and learners with additional needs, some of whom may be learners with EAL. The idea is that well thought-out and planned assessment will inform the planning cycle, and therefore have a positive impact on achieving better outcomes for all learners.

Assessment is a critical aspect of all areas of learning in the Early Years Foundation Stage (DfE, 2014), and is a continuous part of a practitioner's daily routine. In Early Years it is advisable that a variety of assessments be used in different contexts (such as through indoor/outdoor play) in order to gain a more holistic view of the learner. This is especially important with learners who have EAL as they may not fit the accepted criteria of assessment as per the EYFS e-profile. Assessment also provides a basis for discussions with parents about their 'learner's progress and the next steps they need to take' (Daly, Byres and Taylor, 2004: 95). Many Early Years settings carry out a range of assessments even though formal assessment is not required until the end of the foundation stage (Daly et al., 2004) through the achievement of the Early Learning Goals (ELGs). Firstly, we set the scene by discussing the context of assessment for learners with EAL.

Why can assessment of learners with EAL in Early Years be different?

Assessment for learners with EAL in Early Years can be different because they may have language skills in languages other than English which need to be recognised in order to help identify a starting point in language acquisition and tracking progress. It is useful for practitioners to know how long the learner has been used to hearing the English language as it helps them to ascertain whether they have to start right at the beginning, or whether there is some recognition of certain words (such as chocolate, ice cream, coca-cola which are the same in many languages). Safford (2003: 8) and Conteh (2012: 40) suggest that practitioners working with EAL learners have to manage the assessment process in a different way, which is quite a complex issue because of a range of language and cultural backgrounds. This means that assessment used for other learners in the setting may need to be adjusted in terms of its format and criteria to show that the starting point of the learner with EAL is different, and then the tracking of attainment from this shows the value added of learning experiences.

It is therefore important to remember that we need to treat each learner with EAL as a unique individual with specific needs. These learners should be given the time and space to consolidate their learning on what they already know and can do. Learners with EAL may require different contextual opportunities through play with items that they may be familiar with, such as using animal toys, rather than puppets from traditional and multi-cultural tales which maybe unknown to them at this early stage. They may also experience other learning in different contexts, such as mosques, temples, churches and other complementary education, which needs to be valued through relevant activities for these learners. Discussion and involvement with the parents is therefore valuable because it enables a holistic picture of the learner to be built up and an inclusive approach to assessment developed. Next, we begin with some clarity regarding the purpose of assessment.

Purpose of assessment

As noted above, the purpose of assessment is to help practitioners know how well the learner is learning, achieving and progressing through evidence gathered and analysed. Another purpose of assessment can be tracking how learners grow and develop so additional opportunities can be provided (such as greater opportunities to play outdoors if this is an area that learners are unsure of or lack confidence in, or greater opportunities for spoken language activities). Providing additional opportunities like this also helps practitioners to put early interventions in place to support learner development. Assessment also helps practitioners to forward plan individualised needs, like linguistic/cultural needs of a learner with EAL. The EYFS (DfE, 2013b) suggests assessment as a tool by which to analyse an individual learner's development and learning. We need to be clear as to why we are carrying out assessment of a learner. The following are some principles of good practice for practitioners to reflect upon (adapted from QCA, 2000: 8 in Conteh, 2012: 89).

- Be clear about the purposes of assessment, distinguishing summative, formative and diagnostic aims.
- Be sensitive to the learner's first or main other language(s) and heritage culture.
- Take account of how long the learner has been learning English, and the context of this.
- Assess in ways that are appropriate for the learner's age.
- Focus on language, while being aware of the influence of behaviour, attitude and cultural expectations.

Learners with EAL may be at different levels of attainment in speaking, listening, reading and writing, and therefore this is going to have an impact on their starting point in assessment. A useful starting point may be a combination of different types of assessments to suit the context of learning, which we focus on next.

Types of assessment

There are two main categories of assessment: formative assessment and summative assessment. Formative assessment is collection of evidence, its analysis and feedback that is offered as a continuous cycle of improvement and can be undertaken through observation recordings, for example (Palaiologou, 2012: 145). This type of assessment helps one to understand what the learner can and cannot do in order to help them progress to the next level. With an EAL learner, early assessment and profiling is helpful, such as information about their cultural background and what language(s) are spoken or understood. Summative assessment is about the final cycle of attainment in very specific ways like the SATs at the end of Key Stage One. In the EYFS it is a statutory requirement that each learner has a summative assessment (DfE, 2012). We must emphasise that both types of assessment are important and summative assessment is helpful when looking at transitions, especially from one early years setting to another, and approaches to other agencies (Palaiologou, 2012: 146).

For a learner who has EAL, it is important that the planning and types of assessment practitioners undertake are fit for purpose and meet the individual needs of that learner. This implies that planning, delivery and assessment can be promoted through partnership working, where teams or individual practitioners can work flexibly. For example, different practitioners in a setting can observe the same learner with EAL in different contexts at different times in order to identify his/her achievement or where s/he needs further support from a more objective perspective. DfE (2012) suggests this could be done best with parental involvement as part of the assessment process. In addition, Conteh (2012: 87) points out that good planning for 'bilingual and EAL learners' requires 'assessing both their achievements and their attainment'.

What could be the key areas for assessing learners with EAL?

According to NALDIC (2011), there is no national directive that ensures that learners with EAL are assessed differently. This means that learners with EAL can be assessed in the same way as their non-EAL peers, but adjustments in assessments can take place as discussed later in this chapter in order to show progress in attainment. In Early Years the key areas of assessment are all the seven areas of learning within the EYFS (DfE, 2014). Obviously, there are some areas within the EYFS that have greater priority in terms of assessment, such as the prime areas and mathematics.

In our view additional key areas for assessing learners with EAL also include language development, how well they understand a concept or how are they progressing in learning. Conteh (2012: 56) also uses the well-tried KWHL grid to support assessment for learners with EAL. We have adapted this to the Early Years context (see Table 4.1).

Practitioners can plan resources and learning activities similar to those suggested next. Once the practitioners have the data, it is important then to map the next progression of learning activities. It is worth noting that one of the most common errors noted in some literature and by some practitioners is of difficulties of English language comprehension if it is not a learner's first language. So we need to be sensitive to the learner's needs and take care not to make assumptions which could lead to 'unwitting stereotyping or even racism' (Conteh, 2012: 88) when interpreting assessment of learning. Let us now turn to methods of assessment.

Table 4.1 The KWHL grid (adapted from Conteh, 2012: 56)

KWHL grid	Supporting example (through the story of The Very Hungry Caterpillar) – repetitive text
K = what we know	Food item and its colour, shape, taste
W = what we want to find out	Life-cycle of the butterfly – showing growth and changes pictorially
H = how we will find this out	Observing growth and changes of a caterpillar over time
L = what we will learn	How life-cycle changes take place and why

Methods of assessment

For assessment, it is desirable to identify a set of appropriate methods and instruments that provide the necessary information and are refined for use over time to suit the context and the level of the learner. It is important to note that for assessment to be effective in a setting there is no one method that will suit all purposes. In Early Years one main form of assessment for government-registered settings is the e-profile. However, many settings use alternative methods (in addition to the e-profile) to suit their contexts such as the Early Years Outcomes. The most important aspect to remember is that the quality of information gathered and the resulting decisions through planning is paramount. Some of the most popular and useful methods of assessment to support the e-profile for learners with EAL include:

- **Observations** – this is a longstanding tradition in Early Years and involves the skill of observation through play (both indoors and outdoors) and interactions with one another during daily activities and routines. An example of this is, when observing learners with EAL, firstly, are they familiar with the toy they are playing with or is it something new for them? Secondly, if play involves being part of a group or sharing equipment, then what language or gestures are used to support this process? This can be challenging when there is a diverse population of EAL learners.
- **Interviews** – this involves collecting assessment data for each EAL learner that is reported by practitioners regarding the learner's skills and behaviours. Interviews are useful for including the multiple perspectives of parents, practitioners and learners themselves. They are the preferred method for gathering contextual information to clarify a learner's history, cultural background and preferences, and identify specific family priorities (for example, the position the learner in the family, and the impact of this).
- **Basic note-taking** – on post-its or sticky labels regarding immediate observations or learning outcomes, which allows the adjustment of activities for a learner with EAL as they are carried out. These unplanned notes can also help with early interventions of support if required.
- **Specific assessments** – may be useful for parents and outside agencies, meaning that they do not have too much teacher jargon, and can show progression over a period of time. One example could be that certain assessments have a notes section for parents, so that it is easier to decipher meaning in terms of what the evidence shows and how it links to the given area of learning. This in turn is a good basis for parents to compare their learner's activities between their home environment and their setting environment.
- **Annotated photographs** – whereby photos are taken by both practitioners and learners themselves and annotated, then uploaded to the e-profile or used as supporting evidence for observations.

A summary of some of the advantages and disadvantages of each approach is given in Table 4.2, enabling consideration to take place to support practice.

Ongoing assessment forms an integral part of the learning and development process (DfE, 2012: 10) and some literature shows that observational recording techniques with learners with EAL appear to help practitioners. We expand on a few examples of these observational techniques next, but offer a word of caution that such evidence

Table 4.2 Summary of evidence collection tools

Method	Advantages	Disadvantages
Observations	Can be done indoors/outdoors; space and time to do it any time; focused aim; anyone trained to observe	Time set aside for analysing data; if the aim is not specified it can be difficult to interpret data; interpreter bias if not trained or aware of EAL needs specifically
Interviews	Multiple stakeholder perspectives gathered, allowing triangulation; lots of information available prior to interviews; probing possible to dig deep	Sampling; interpreting triangulated responses accurately; cultural bias
Basic note-taking	Easy data collection method; easy recording on post-its for example; easy for first order synthesis; unplanned learning recorded 'on the hoof'	Not rich/thick data for interpretation; hard to inform practice for the future with limited, unsubstantiated data
Specific assessments	Other stakeholders can be involved, such as parents; recording information using latest ICT tools/apps; fostering true setting–parents partnerships for the benefit of EAL learners	Difficulty of generating interest amongst EAL learner parents to get involved to share information; making sense of information (may be too wide and diverse) for action planning
Annotated photographs	Practitioners can take photos of EAL learners' activities; learners themselves taking photos using an iPad, for example	Time-consuming activity, especially annotating the evidence that shows progress/attainment of learners with EAL

gathering forms only part of a number of techniques to obtain a holistic picture of a learner's learning and development. According to Palaiologou (2012: 58), the three types of observation are unstructured observations (where you are the participant observer), structured observations (where you are a non-participant observer) and semi-structured observations.

Observation as an assessment tool

One of the most used assessment tools in Early Years is observations in different contexts through both learner- and practitioner-initiated activities. Palaiologou (2012: 45) uses Carr's (2001) concept developed in New Zealand's Te Whaariki curriculum which has five goals: well-being; belonging; contribution; communication and exploration. This model is useful for a setting where there are learners with EAL in order to carry out effective observation and assessment because this is a bicultural curriculum. But we do recognise that there may be other models too. In Table 4.3, we suggest behaviours to keep in mind for learners who have EAL in relation to the Te Whaariki curriculum.

Table 4.3 The Te Whaariki model (adapted from Carr, 2001, cited in Palaiologou, 2012: 45)

The strands of the Te Whaariki curriculum	The behaviour identified within activities for learners with EAL in Early Years
Belonging	Taking an interest
Well-being	Being involved
Exploration	Persisting with difficulty, challenges and uncertainty
Communication	Expressing a point of view or feeling
Contribution	Taking responsibility

Some thoughts that could support practice in an Early Years setting include:

- When working with an EAL learner, try to observe their behaviour against one of the five strands in this model.
- What is noticed, and what could be the reasons for it?
- Now try repeating this task with a learner-initiated play-based activity – indoor or outdoor.
- How is the information gained different from that from the first task, and why?

So, for example, in daily practice, observe when a learner takes an interest in an activity or becomes involved in it over a sustained period of time. Carr (2001) calls these learning episodes 'learning stories' (cited in Palaiologou, 2012: 46), which may offer practitioners opportunities for further planning of activities, especially if aimed at learners with EAL. What we add is that these learning stories need to be contextually balanced in that they need to be practitioner/learner-led and practitioner/learner-initiated in both the indoor and outdoor environments through all areas of learning. As Palaiologou (2012: 55) notes, becoming a skilled observer is complex and challenging, requiring individuals to 'overcom[e] personal emotional boundaries'. Thus it is important to spend time and effort in observing planning, and this can involve parents of learners with EAL to further share information and to promote partnership. We consider a few examples and scenarios of assessing learners with EAL in the next section.

How to assess learners with EAL

Good Early Years practice is founded on principles and processes involving sound observation, assessment and planning (DfE, 2012). What we need to focus on in Early Years is a more consistent approach to observation, assessment, recording and reporting to inform us with regard to what to offer our learners. This will remind us to refocus our emphasis on the individual learner, who is a unique person. We begin by looking at what kind of data can be used to see how well a learner with EAL is making progress in Early Years. Strategies to begin this process and give an initial contextual starting point include the following:

- Write the name and age of the learner.
- What do the learner's records say, including attainment data?
- Scrutinise one of their activities?

- Observe the learner in the class with their peers.
- Talk to practitioners currently working with the learner.
- Interviewing/spending time with the learner.
- Write a summary and evaluation of the current provision made.
- What are the recommendations for future provision (practical interventions that will enhance the progress of the learner)?

The context of any kind of assessment needs to be taken into consideration, as we know that unless learners are fully comfortable in the setting our results may not be accurate. For learners with EAL, one of the best contexts in Early Years is structured and unstructured play, whereby the learners have the freedom to be in charge of their learning journey without a specific end product. Next we move on to the specifics of exactly what kind of data to record, how to collect it and how to analyse it for progression of learners with EAL through the process of observation and questioning.

Case study 4.1

Amisha is a girl aged five in a reception setting, of mixed heritage and the second child of the family. Earlier records had shown that she was shy in playing with other learners in the setting. So the task was to observe Amisha for 10 minutes when she was drawing in the creative area of the setting with the aim of seeing her social development. A practitioner helped in observing her when she was interacting with a peer. The dialogue between the two learners was recorded and analysis of it showed that Amisha, with the helpful probing of closed and open questions by the practitioner, was able to work collaboratively with her peer. The practitioner then started to ask the learners about the picture of a mango that Amisha had drawn, in terms of its size, shape and colour, to encourage conversation to aid the progression of both learners. Here, with the help of the practitioner, Amisha was making sense of the task to draw and describe the mango. Both learners were able to show evidence of co-operating to learn about drawing the fruit. Amisha was progressing at her own level and pace, and with more learning opportunities, extending her vocabulary and skills.

Case study 4.1 shows one example of how observational data was used to support questioning in an activity to help probe the learner's understanding. With participant observation, this can be a simple and immediate tool, but the difficulty is in its use as a whole setting activity, especially when we are note-taking as we observe and then try to make sense of the data soon afterwards. So one needs to find out what kind of recording method a setting uses for this type of observation.

Drawing on theory about analysis, Palaiologou (2012: 85) defines analysis as being 'valid explanation' (based on behaviour observed), or 'faulty explanation' (maybe biased as it is formed from your personal opinion) or 'conclusions' (made from a judgement based on collective observations). So the aim of analysis is to have valid explanation which forms a conclusion from observation and is not biased. How can we ensure that what we were observing between Amisha and her peer was truly based on observation to form non-judgemental conclusion? This is worth debating with others. Case study 4.2 illustrates how the structure of assessments used in the setting may need to be adjusted for learners with EAL.

Case study 4.2

Gurmeet was a new bilingual practitioner in a nursery setting. Her first language was Punjabi in addition to Hindi, Urdu and English. She carried out some assessments jointly with the nursery practitioner so that she was clear as to what she was looking for and what she should be making a note of. However, when carrying out assessments alone, she realised that there was no direct translation for some of the English terminology used in the first languages of some of the learners.

Gurmeet was observing the practitioner carrying out an observation of a learner with EAL in the setting home corner which had been set up as a supermarket. Kumar was five years old and from a Hindu–Punjabi background. He was conversing with peers about what he was going to buy in the supermarket. Kumar picked up a potato, pretended to cut it and eat it, and said 'chickoo' to his peer. At this point the practitioner intervened and asked Kumar, 'What is in your hand?' Kumar replied by saying 'chickoo' as he continued to pretend to eat it. The practitioner shook her head and said to Kumar, 'This is a potato.' At this point Kumar looked confused and repeated 'chickoo' whilst holding it out to the practitioner. The practitioner, through conversations with Gurmeet, later found out that a chickoo is an Indian fruit which looks just like a potato. In Gurmeet's view, this observation led to assessments being carried out which did not provide an accurate picture of those learners such as Kumar who have EAL.

Case study 4.2 highlights that practitioners need to be aware that assessment documents are there to be used as a guide only. At times they will need to be adjusted slightly in terms of their targets to show progression, and sometimes they may need to be redone in a different context to allow the learner the best possible chance of showing progress. This is particularly the case with learners with EAL as the progress they make initially may be slower compared with the rest of the cohort due to a language barrier, yet this progress needs to be highlighted – which can only happen, as good practice suggests, if targets are adjusted to show the evidence, or that language is tweaked on assessment schedules.

The importance of adjusting assessments for learners with EAL

What may be helpful is to look at the help that can be available within the setting or externally to support the activities and assessment for EAL learners. Roberts (1995) suggests that whatever the reason for assessment, it always raises questions in regard to a learner's well-being and self-esteem, and how individuals see themselves as learners. In the case of learners with EAL, good practice is all about their well-being and self-esteem being the initial priority – especially if they are new arrivals. They need time to settle into a new environment with new resources and new expectations before they can be assessed against set criteria.

Practitioners should also not assume that if learners with EAL seem to have 'an inability to speak English, it is automatically a sign of special needs' (NAA, 2007: 1). What is needed here are additional observations to be carried out discreetly both indoors and outdoors through play to see if the lack of English language is essentially just a language barrier or whether there is something more. But we recognise how this can have an impact on a practitioner's time and workload, thus requiring sensitive management. It is also worth other practitioners in the setting carrying out observations too in order to gain a more objective perspective, as sometimes practitioners can be too close to the EAL learners.

Why should assessment be meaningful?

In one way or another, all Early Years assessments involve a process of gathering information about learners in an attempt to better understand and support their learning and development. It is more accurate to say that we assess young learners' behaviours, skills, competencies, confidences, preferences and interactions than to say that we assess the learners themselves. Assessment results can describe some informative details of what learners know and can do, but can 'never fully portray who they are as individuals' (OSPI, 2008: 11). Meaningful assessment involves thoughtful choices on the part of all Early Years practitioners regarding the many purposes, types, methods and instruments available to assist us in getting to know our learners very well. For example, sitting in the imaginative play area whilst learners go into role can provide valuable information especially for learners with EAL as it gives an insight into their use of resources as well as their language and social development.

Assessment in Early Years needs to be meaningful owing to the contextual nature of learning through play. The main form of assessment is the Early Years Foundation Stage Profile (EYFSP) which requires all practitioners who work in Early Years settings to assess learners against the seventeen ELGs (DfE, 2014). The EYFSP is 'an inclusive assessment, capable of capturing a wide range of learning and development outcomes' (DfE, 2013a: 12). Each practitioner is required to use their judgement to decide whether learners achieve the terms emerging, expected or exceeded in relation to the ELGs by the end of their reception year. The e-profile itself is an electronic tool that collates information throughout the Early Years phase in order to judge how well the ELGs are achieved by learners by the end of the reception year, and is used by government-registered maintained Early Years settings. Many settings also use additional assessment (such as tracking grids or own setting designed grids) to support the e-profile so that there is a more holistic view of the learner. This is good practice in the case of learners with EAL whereby more observations through play may be necessary than just a checklist type of assessment.

The implications of assessment for learners with EAL in Early Years

Complete and meaningful assessment in early childhood necessitates an understanding of family context, including getting to know family language and culture, gathering developmental information from parents, and conducting home visits with parent approval.

This principle applies to all learners and families, but is especially critical for learners whose families may not share the language or some of the economic advantages of the dominant culture. Understanding family expectations and experience places a learner's behaviour in context and can prevent harmful decisions that result from misinterpretation of assessment data (NAEYC, 2005). Daly *et al.* (2004: 95) suggest that through the information gained from assessments, practitioners need to 'have realistic expectations' of their learners, which is essential for learners with EAL as their expectations need to be coherent with their life experiences to date, especially if they are new arrivals.

Assessment should be linguistically appropriate, recognising that to some extent all assessments are measures of language. Regardless of whether an assessment is intended to measure early reading skills, knowledge of colour names or learning potential, assessment results are easily confused by language proficiency, especially for learners who come from home backgrounds with limited exposure to English, for whom the assessment would essentially be an assessment of their English proficiency. Each learner's first- and second-language development should be taken into account when determining appropriate assessment methods and in interpreting the meaning of assessment results. Parents should be a valued source of assessment information as they know their learner best. Because of the fallibility of direct measures of young learners, assessments should include multiple sources of evidence, especially reports from parents and practitioners. Assessment results should be shared with parents as part of an ongoing process that involves parents in their learner's education.

Potential challenges in assessing learners with EAL

One of the challenges faced by practitioners in Early Years settings is what happens to learners who still remain within the context of the EYFS after the end of the reception year, which may be the case for learners with EAL. The issue here is how to assess learners in Key Stage One, when the e-profile ends at the end of the reception year. Some settings have created interim assessments to support the transition phase between reception and Year 1. However, this would imply that practitioners in both Key Stage One and Early Years need to be familiar with the assessments used across both phases, which in turn has an impact on training and associated costs. Nevertheless, despite the guidance from the EYFS and EYP there can be a concern that over-assessment takes place as the impact of greater accountability by the practitioners is called for. Another challenge is the issue of time in relation to areas of learning. Setting priorities at times dictate which area of learning should be the key focus, and therefore other areas can be overlooked, especially if this is linked to a forthcoming Ofsted inspection, as illustrated by Case study 4.3.

Case study 4.3

Jasmine was a reception practitioner in the early stages of her career. Her setting was due an Ofsted inspection during the academic year, and therefore all practitioners were focusing on assessment as it was a key area of development from the previous inspection. As a result of this, Jasmine spent a lot of time carrying out assessments and gathering evidence in relation to certain key areas of learning, such as Communication and Language, Literacy, and Maths. Twenty per cent of her class were learners with EAL, some of whom were at the very early stages of English language acquisition. However, owing to the pressure of the imminent Ofsted inspection, Jasmine focused on carrying out her assessments on a weekly basis. After six weeks, she began to analyse the data gathered, and found that in the case of some learners with EAL, very little or no progress could be identified. Her initial thoughts were that they had a form of special need. However, after seeking advice from the Special Needs Co-ordinator (SENCO), she began to create opportunities for play without being present to make notes for assessment. She began to intervene in and out of activities, and also to observe at a distance. Jasmine realised that by giving the learners with EAL time and space to settle in without her constant presence, they began a dialogue with other learners in the class who were more proficient in English as they felt they were not being watched. In addition Jasmine realised that discreet assessments also gave her more complete data, which showed greater progress than at times when she felt the need to encourage learners to work with her for the sake of keeping the assessment momentum going for the forthcoming Ofsted inspection.

The whole nature of Early Years puts the learner at the heart of the process. Case study 4.3 clearly demonstrates that good practice is about giving thinking and conversation time to learners with EAL to explore and investigate various activities. It is advisable to see how opportunities for assessment in the setting could be integrated so that the focus on Ofsted priorities can still occur without it overtaking everything; otherwise the progression of learners with needs like those who have EAL can be hampered. In addition to this, there is also the consideration of learners with EAL who have not achieved all the ELGs. Sometimes practitioners may also feel that with the pressure of assessments and accountability, there may not be enough time in the setting for opportunities to achieve the ELGs through the different areas of learning. Case study 4.4 shows the worry caused to a practitioner if the ELGs are not achieved by the end of the Early Years phase.

Case study 4.4

Mohit, a Nepalese learner, was a new arrival in the reception setting halfway through the year. Prior to his arrival, he had no formal pre-setting experience. However, he was a very sociable learner with some understanding of some basic words in English which enabled him to join in with his peers in play activities. As a result of his late school start, his e-profile was not fully completed by the end of the reception year. He had also not achieved all the ELGs. His practitioner was worried about his transition into Year 1 with such limited opportunities and experience.

Case study 4.4 highlights the reality that not all learners with EAL will achieve all the ELGs by the end of the reception phase. What is important is how collaboration takes place with the Year 1 team to ensure, firstly, that progression is smooth for the individual, but also that assessment links are clear so that natural progression takes place. In discussion with lead practitioners, it may be worth considering continuing with the e-profile for the first few weeks of the new term in Year 1 before the transition to National Curriculum assessments takes place.

Practical strategies to support these challenges

Following are some suggestions of good practice to help overcome some of the challenges above, as adapted from Sood and Mistry (2011) and from our observations of practitioners in a variety of Early Years settings.

- For learners who have EAL you could continue with the e-profile (or other forms of assessment) into Year 1 for the autumn term.
- Make sure that the chosen assessment tool works for the context of the setting through managing quality and continuity.
- There needs to be a common understanding of the assessments carried out so that they look familiar, which makes it easier for practitioners to use them in their settings.
- All practitioners in the setting working with learners of EAL need to be trained to carry out assessments; this helps to provide different perspectives.
- Making sure that time for assessments is planned into the weekly planning. Sometimes assessments will happen spontaneously, which is the nature of Early Years.
- It is also advisable to have another practitioner around (if possible) when carrying out assessments so that they can deal with minor interruptions in order to give focused time.
- Parents need to be valued and respected as a source of information for assessment – the key here is good relationships.

In summary, the main points to be aware of in supporting the assessment of learners with EAL are focused on pedagogical and pragmatic reasons. So a team approach is advocated, which is a natural form of set-up in EY, to devise an assessment tool that is understood by all, easy to apply and easy to interpret. Involving parents as external observers of quality control may be a good strategy.

Examples of assessment templates

Rather than suggesting lots of assessment templates that are unique to a given context, we have suggested web links for various Early Years assessments. This should offer a starting point, especially if practitioners are new to assessment, but we are mindful that there are many more templates.

http://earlylearningconsultancy.co.uk/summarising-learning-and-development/
www.earlylearninghq.org.uk/class-management/observation-and-assessment/
www.egfl.org.uk/categories/teaching/assess/found.html
www.eriding.net/eyfs/oap_cd.shtml

www.gloucestershire.gov.uk/extra/article/109475/Early-Years-Foundation-Stage-Assessment
www.gloucestershire.gov.uk/extra/article/115961/EYFS-Summative-Development-Record
www.thegrid.org.uk/learning/foundation/eyfs/
www.thegrid.org.uk/learning/foundation/resources/

These suggested assessment templates need to be supported with reflective comments in order to serve a useful purpose in terms of understanding learners better. When practitioners have a better understanding of their learners, they have a greater responsibility to 'foster and develop their learning further' (Nutbrown and Carter, 2010: 113). Whatever the combination of assessments used, good practice tells us that there needs to be a variety of contextual activities, both indoor and outdoor, through as many different areas of learning as possible. This is so that learners, especially those who have EAL, are not disadvantaged by pencil and paper methods alone. There also needs to be some clear guidance on how and when key assessments should be carried out in terms of an assessment policy. The policy should show the progression between Early Years and Key Stage One, and the rest of the age phases. Good practice is made up of a balance of assessment approaches creatively developed by all practitioners.

Summary

This chapter has considered a range of assessment approaches for learners with EAL. Before any assessment can begin for a new arrival with EAL, practitioners give them time to become familiar with the routines and expectations of a setting. There are different types of assessment that map the learning progression of each learner, captured through formative and summative approaches. The assessment methods used by practitioners need to be more personalised and sensitively undertaken, and appropriate judgements made for learners with EAL. Here, ethical ways of carrying out observations as one tool for assessing progress are particularly important. The chapter also introduced some practical ways in which practitioners can use assessment process to support and promote learning for learners with EAL. Different varieties of evidence gained through assessment for effective learning of learners with EAL may be quite challenging and this will require careful analytical skills to ensure that learners with EAL achieve and attain. Good understanding about assessment is necessary when dealing with parents so that they can assist the setting in this important process.

Reflective questions

- How can a setting's assessments be adjusted to suit learners with EAL to show they are making progress?
- Reflect on the advantages and disadvantages of different assessments that support data collection for the e-profile or Early Years Outcomes for learners with EAL.
- Reflect on the importance of context when assessments are carried out for EAL learners, and what the role of practitioners and peers is in this process.

References

Carr, M. (2001) *Assessment in early childhood settings*. London: Sage.

Conteh, J. (2012) *Teaching bilingual and EAL learners in primary schools*. London: Sage and Learning Matters, pp. 87–100.

Daly, M., Byres, E. and Taylor, W. (2004) *Early Years management in practice*. Abingdon: Heinemann.

Department for Education (DfE) (2012) *Statutory framework for the Early Years Foundation Stage (EYFS)*. London: DfE.

Department for Education (DfE) (2013a) *Assessment and reporting arrangements: Early Years Foundation Stage*. London: Standards and Testing Agency.

Department for Education (DfE) (2013b) *National Curriculum assessments: Early Years Foundation Stage Profile*. London: Standards and Testing Agency.

Department for Education (DFE) (2014) *Statutory framework for the Early Years Foundation Stage (EYFS)*. London: DFE, https://www.gov.uk/government/uploads/system/uploads/attachment_data/file/299391/DFE-00337-2014.pdf (accessed April 2014).

National Assessment Agency (NAA) (2007) *Guidance notes: assessing children who are learning English as an additional language*. London: National Assessment Agency.

National Association for Language Development in the Curriculum (NALDIC) (2011) Is there a nationally agreed EAL assessment system? www.naldic.org.uk/eal-teaching-and-learning/faqs/ass-faq (accessed June 2014).

National Association for the Education of Young Children (NAEYC) with National Association of Early Childhood Specialists in State Departments of Education (NAECS/SDE) (2005) *Joint position statement in supplement to early childhood curriculum, assessment, and program evaluation: building an effective, accountable system in programs for children birth through age 8*. Washington, DC: NAEYC.

Nutbrown, C. and Carter, C. (2010) The tools of assessment: watching and learning, in G. Pughand and B. Duffy (eds), *Contemporary issues in the Early Years*. London: Sage, pp. 109–22.

Office of Superintendent for Public Instruction (OSPI) (2008) *A guide to assessment in early childhood: infancy to age eight*. Washington, DC: OSPI.

Palaiologou, I. (2012) *Child observation for the Early Years*, 2nd edn. London: Sage/Learning Matters.

Quality and Curriculum Authority (QCA) (2000) *A language in common: assessing English as an additional language*. QCA Publications, http://media.education.gov.uk/assets/files/pdf/a/a%20language%20in%20common%20assessing%20eal.pdf (accessed 29 September 2013).

Roberts, R. (1995) *Self-esteem and successful early learning*. London: Hodder and Stoughton.

Safford, K. (2003) *Teachers and pupils in the big picture: seeing real children in routinized assessment*. Watford: National Association for Language Development in the Curriculum (NALDIC).

Sood, K. and Mistry, M. (2011) English as an Additional Language: is there a need to embed cultural values and beliefs in institutional practice? *Education 3–13: International Journal of Primary, Elementary and Early Years Education*, 39(2): 203–15.

Chapter 5

Planning for learners with EAL in Early Years

'The function of education is to teach one to think intensively and to think critically. Intelligence plus character – that is the goal of true education.'

Martin Luther King, Jr (Unique teaching resources, 2014)

The aims of this chapter

- To offer a starting point in planning for learners with EAL
- To be aware of what planning in Early Years needs to include for learners with EAL
- To consider how planning can be adjusted to meet the needs of learners with EAL to show progress in attainment

Overview

Effective planning is a key feature of any good practitioner's work to ensure the well-being, happiness and safeguarding of all learners, but especially for those who have EAL and who may be more vulnerable in a new environment. This vulnerability may arise from the learners not understanding English. This chapter begins by briefly linking the Early Years Foundation Stage (EYFS) curriculum and planning before reflecting on some considerations prior to planning. Then we look at the usefulness of planning sheets in our daily practice. We know that good planning is based on genuine partnerships through listening to and learning from diverse populations with diverse cultural experiences to share; therefore the next section will look at how deploying diverse practitioners can support the planning process. We then move on to the role of Ofsted in supporting planning and the integral link between planning and assessment, before focusing on how planning can be tailored to meet the needs of learners with EAL through illustrative case studies from Early Years settings. Next we look at how to adapt the planning cycle specifically for learners with EAL. Then we reflect on potential barriers to planning for learners with EAL before finally offering ideas such as planning templates for aspects of planning that can be adapted to the specific contextual needs of the setting.

Key words: planning, EYFS curriculum, differentiation, areas of learning

Introduction

It is useful to keep in mind that the context of planning in Early Years can be different to that of the rest of the setting (especially if the Early Years phase is part of a primary setting), and this will also vary between settings as a result of the contextual nature of such learning in comparison with the National Curriculum. This is because learning in Early Years is through foci such as play and themed learning opportunities that link to areas of learning rather than through subject-based learning. Therefore the planning process for learners with EAL requires careful consideration of the EYFS curriculum context. It needs to be scaffolded to enable access to the curriculum through links to the four principles of the EYFS (DfE, 2014) through initial learner observations, in addition, taking account of guidance from NALDIC (2012) and Ofsted (2012).

The EYFS and planning

Planning in Early Years encompasses seven areas of learning which are seen as being developmental and very much centred on the philosophy of indoor and outdoor play as well as learning through first-hand experiences. Indeed, the EYFS (DfE, 2014) recognises the continuum of learning from zero to the end of the reception year and emphasises the importance of learning and development in terms of stage, not age (Drake, 2010: xii). In the EYFS the three prime areas of Physical Development, Personal Social Emotional Development, and Communication and Language are seen to be the foundations of learning, with the four specific areas of Mathematics, Literacy, Understanding the World, and Expressive Arts and Design building on these foundations. According to the EYFS (DfE, 2012: 4–7), 'in planning and guiding children's activities, practitioners must reflect on the different ways that learners learn and reflect these in their practice'. It is imperative, then, to have good knowledge and understanding of how learners learn and develop, and therefore secure knowledge of each area of learning is paramount. This means that where there are learners with EAL in the setting, practitioners need to be mindful of their specific needs in their planning and use of resources.

As this chapter is about meeting the planned needs of learners with EAL, it is important to plan for their specific cultural, linguistic and educational needs. In that respect, then, we must plan for the holistic nature of learners' learning, as learning can happen in both planned and unplanned ways, which is considered next.

Some considerations prior to planning

It is useful to remind ourselves of some of the effective ways learners learn by drawing on Fisher's (1996) ideas that support the thinking behind the planning process. Here, the suggestion is that learners are seen to be active, organised in their own learning experiences, using language and interacting with others (Fisher, cited in Drake, 2010: xvi). With respect to language for learners with EAL, it is important to acknowledge that where a learner with EAL chooses to use their own home language, this will have implications for planning and resources, especially if they have not used certain resources such as play dough or stickle bricks before. This means that learners may not know what they are supposed to do with these resources unless they are modelled by practitioners or peers.

Another aspect to keep in mind prior to planning is creativity and imagination which are the linchpin of how learners engage with the world around them and this is actively promoted in the EYFS (DfE, 2014). Through offering open-ended learning opportunities, practitioners can observe how different groups of learners interact with each other, their surroundings and other practitioners. Effective planning and an appropriately resourced environment lead to high quality learning. This may also require practitioners to facilitate open-ended learning opportunities and new ways of working that are inclusive for all learners, especially for those who have EAL. For example, Sailesh and his sister Tina had just returned from a visit to their village in Punjab, India. They had lots of stories to tell their fellow learners. So the practitioner planned a creative session where she displayed some of the photographs of their visit, annotating them by using iPads to capture and display the images and text. Both learners had lots to say and the practitioner set up a question and answer session to make this happen. There was much spontaneous learning and fun in the activities planned for the learners, with much new knowledge and understanding gained about the Punjab village where Sailesh and Tina's grandparents lived.

Drake (2010) suggests the importance of taking time to share one's thinking with the learner through playful learning alongside them. Through modelling skills and ideas, connections in a learner's learning can be made which is not just essential for all learners, but especially for those who have EAL, as their home language and cultural context can be different. Of course, we need to judge when to step aside and let the learner be independent, but also to know when to intervene to support them in making choices and decisions as and when necessary (Woods, 2013). As Drake (2010: 6) notes, the stage of a learner's development is 'rooted in observation-based assessments'. So the implications of this for planning mean that practitioners need to continue to carefully plan the provision, giving thought to all areas of learning and the full range of needs within the setting (Drake, 2010: 7). One way this can be done is by different practitioners in the setting carrying out initial observations in different indoor and outdoor contexts in order to gain an objective holistic view of the learner. We turn next to planning learning and suggest that most settings use some form of template or planning sheets to develop their planning, in the short, medium and long term.

Using planning sheets

Planning sheets, pro-formas or templates are one way of recording evidence that shows learners' developmental progress through an identification of their needs, interests and the understanding of curriculum knowledge and pedagogy over a period of time. Prior knowledge of learners should be embedded in planning to ensure that learning is aimed at the right level, and progression in learning and development is evident. Planning is also informed by observations, general tracking and both formal and informal assessments (see Chapter 4 on assessment). In a busy setting it can be a challenge to move away from the templates or schemes of work, so practitioners need to be flexible and creative to capture the spontaneity of the learning environment and guided by a learner's interests (Woods, 2013), which can be different for those learners who have EAL. An example of differences that we should be mindful of is the fact that not all learners with EAL will have similar experiences to those of other learners in the setting, such as going to the cinema (if all movies are in English), going to a local McDonalds (as it may not have halal food for those who only eat halal meat), or attending the birthday parties of peers in the setting (especially if they are used to family being at birthdays rather than their peers).

However, the distinctiveness of planning for learners who have EAL in Early Years comes from the type and breadth of strategies which build upon their prior knowledge, experiences and language acquisition needs. This implies a dual focus on content and language demands. Within the EYFS (DfE, 2014), the importance of personalised learning is highlighted even more through the seven areas of learning and play. To ensure that learners with EAL reach their potential, learning and teaching approaches through observations to inform planning must continue to be deployed. This will ensure access to the curriculum at a cognitively appropriate level and the best opportunities for maximum language development and connections between areas of learning, as shown through Case studies 5.1 and 5.2.

Case study 5.1

Shobna, a confident five-year-old Gujerati girl, was observed by a practitioner in role play using resource boxes containing equipment for a Post Office. Shobna uses English and Gujerati words equally in her conversation with her non-EAL friend, who seems to understand what Shobna is trying to say and accepts the direction of play. The practitioner just uses a basic observation sheet and had not planned for this dual conversation account, but makes a note of which words were used, and also whether this mixed use of languages hindered the flow of role play in any way. The practitioner became part of the learner–practitioner dialogue in the role play, thus supporting learning. However, this dialogue was not recorded on the observation sheet and therefore key information had been missed. The practitioner also realised that when it came to planning, the information on her observation sheet was very descriptive and therefore it took time to find the key message, which was that by allowing for free flow of activity, language as a barrier was not an issue for learning through play for Shobna. From reflecting on this case study, the practitioner adjusted her observation sheet to ensure that she only made key notes to help inform her future planning for Shobna.

Case study 5.1 suggests that having the time and space to think the unthinkable should be allowed (Woods, 2013). It is also important to see Shobna take centre stage in her play scenario which gives hope to practitioners that reflective journeys are an acceptable part of learning. As Moss and Petrie (2002: 185) note, seeing where the journey takes Shobna, 'opens up new understanding and new ways of seeing' for practitioners. Learners of different nationalities, gender and ability/disability will make their own sense of what they are doing when playing and will equally have different interpretations. 'Meaning-making and strategies of doing things' (Taguchi, 2010: 34) therefore need to be interpreted in the same diverse and different way by the practitioners. Practitioners then need to reflect on the information in front of them and to adjust aspects of observation sheets if necessary to ensure that they have the information they need for future planning to be progressive for the learner. With some inexperienced practitioners, as in Case study 5.2, we explore how they can be supported by an experienced mentor in meeting the needs of new arrivals with limited English.

Case study 5.2

Abbu is a mixed-heritage Malaysian male, with an English mother and Malayan father. The family has recently arrived from Malaysia. At the nursery setting, Abbu likes painting, listening to stories when puppets are used and playing with animal toys (small world). He finds speaking English difficult and is therefore very shy with both learners and practitioners. The newly qualified practitioner does not feel comfortable talking with the class about mixed heritage so as not to give stereotypical messages, so she sought the support of the Early Years leader in the setting. The Early Years leader observed Abbu in indoor and outdoor play, and shared her notes from the observation with the practitioner. She then advised the practitioner to include play activities in her planning sheets that involved small world, with homes and people to assess Abbu's spoken language. The practitioner was also advised to plan an activity which discussed the people who live in our home through the use of photographs, and to let the learners lead the discussion to see if a mixed-heritage background caused any stereotypical views from the group. From the outcome of these activities, the Early Years leader advised the practitioner to adjust aspects of her planning sheet to show change as learners can be unpredictable in their thoughts and understanding.

Case study 5.2 shows that it is important to seek the advice of more experienced practitioners in the setting in order to create the best possible learning opportunities. It also shows how important it is to use the information from observations to plan the next steps of learning. Farmer (2002: 141) offers some examples of using dolls with stories to tell in order to better understand diversity, and suggests that using Persona dolls to tell a story must portray 'accurate content, be well researched and positively presented' (Farmer, 2002: 144). It is important to challenge existing stereotypes, and learners in Early Years settings seem to do this naturally through play. Therefore it is helpful to draw on the diverse community where possible to hear their stories, and memories and view photographs in first-hand discussions. We believe such sharing of stories helps to foster good understanding of cultural diversity. But as Gaine (1995) observes, where there is a less diverse community, practitioners will still have some way to go to address perceived stereotypes, prejudice and discrimination. Where there is diverse staffing, their expertise and knowledge can be maximised to strengthen EAL learners' and other learners' experiences.

Deploying diverse practitioners to support planning

Planning in Early Years is about meeting young learners' needs so that they can learn creatively in such ways as through play in order to develop skills and knowledge across the three prime and four specific areas of learning in the EYFS. According to NALDIC (2012), guidance for inspectors on what to look for in EAL teaching and learning during Ofsted inspections has been somewhat brief. Ofsted (2012) suggests that specialist EAL support should be available for new arrivals from qualified practitioners who have received appropriate training and support. More advanced learners of English should have continuing support in line with their varying needs as they develop competencies over time (Ofsted, 2012: 4). However, many settings are not in a position to have this kind of specialist support because of recruitment problems and financial constraints. One example of good practice therefore is where all practitioners have shared ownership of supporting learners with EAL. This has to be actively led and managed across the whole setting system by experienced Early Years leaders.

More specifically, diverse staff can support planning by, firstly, being involved as a key member of the Early Years team, secondly, assertively demonstrating that they have specific knowledge, understanding and skills to share in supporting learners with EAL, and, thirdly, the team acknowledging that through teamwork and collegial sharing, inclusivity is demonstrated to all.

Ofsted and planning in Early Years

Throughout this book we draw upon Ofsted's evidence to support our analysis of the needs of learners with EAL. Ofsted inspectors are the eyes and ears of quality assurance in education in the Early Years. But each setting is different: they have their own history and context, and therefore, must continue to remain steadfast in their vision as excellent educators for their learners and their community. Ofsted (2012) have identified some features of good practice that they look for during inspections regarding provision for learners, such as:

- specialist teaching support for newer arrivals,
- continuing support for more advanced EAL learners,
- monitoring EAL learner attainment and progress,
- assessing EAL learners' proficiency and literacy in their first language and establishing prior knowledge and experience, and
- regular training for all practitioners on the needs of EAL learners.

It is advisable for practitioners to show examples of these features in their planning. Therefore we now look at these five suggestions of good practice in some detail through the ideas below to support practice.

Specialist teaching support for newer arrivals

Where possible, a good specialist heading support for new arrivals can help to settle the learner with EAL quickly, act in translation, and help foster good home–setting links. If this is not possible within the setting, then it may be possible to communicate with nearby settings to see how resources can be shared to support this process. For example, in a private urban nursery setting with 60 per cent learners who have EAL, the policy was for parents to be part of the induction period to settle their learners. In this context, the practitioners worked alongside parents who were expected to stay until their learner was comfortable and secure, especially in the first two weeks – which allowed practitioners to gain key information to support the learning and teaching process. The learners with EAL and their families were allocated a key worker initially to help with the settling-in process. This was essential in a setting that did not have an allocated EAL co-ordinator. However, we do realise that this kind of support is not available in most settings, and therefore practitioners could seek support from more experienced practitioners, or from settings with a higher percentage of learners with EAL to help support practice.

Continuing support for more advanced learners

Not all learners with EAL are in the early stages of English language development. The specific support for these more advanced learners of EAL can include being in higher ability groups, use of collaborative conversations with more able peers, free flow play with practitioner intervention, and regular observations to challenge them further. For example, in a reception setting, the learners were grouped by ability for Literacy and Mathematics. The practitioner did this to help her meet the needs of the learners more precisely. This was especially important for those learners with EAL of which there were only three in a group of twenty-four. The practitioner was worried that the EAL learners should not be isolated learners or overlooked in any way. These learners had overcome the language barrier (which was identified through assessment and observations – see Chapter 4) and were therefore placed in the higher group for both Literacy and Mathematics as per their ability, to ensure that they were challenged sufficiently.

Monitoring EAL attainment and progress

In effective settings, at the heart of monitoring and evaluation procedures are effective structures and systems (Mistry and Sood, 2011). This means that a systematic approach to the collection and recording of information in planning is required (Hopkins, 1994). Examples in Early Years include noting how learners with EAL use their first language during activities and the impact of this on practitioner planning. Mistry and Sood (2011) found that awareness and ownership of all practitioners in the use of a monitoring system that enables learners with EAL to progress have to be tracked more concisely if targeted support is to be developed. In a different study involving learners in a nursery setting, digital photo displays of their day's activity were used as visual clues to help learners with EAL in becoming more confident in speaking English (Ofsted, 2009). Another example from Mistry and Sood (2011) suggests that sharing their EYFS profile tracking data for their EAL learners helped practitioners to better plan personalised activities for these individuals. Ofsted also note that in settings with a high EAL learner population, there is a need for the setting's development plan to have 'clear objectives and strategies for the needs of EAL learners' (Ofsted, 2010: 5).

Assessing learners' proficiency in Literacy within their first language and establishing prior knowledge and experience

The planning process starts by measuring a learner's proficiency in English language through their first language. This can be done initially through observations and conversations which can be used to reflect on the learning taking place and what could be developed next for the learner and for the development of pedagogy. For example, a newly qualified practitioner in a reception setting decided to follow Nazia's interest in the outdoor learning environment attached to the reception setting. Nazia is a four-year-old female who has recently arrived from a small village in Afghanistan. The practitioner observed Nazia fill a small plastic container of water and carry it across the outdoor area several times on her head; she was then joined by two other peers who pretend to do the same. Her peers attempted to balance the containers on their heads several times, but could not do it as successfully as Nazia. They asked Nazia how she does it. She laughed and carried on. When the practitioner asked, 'Can I join in?', Nazia said 'Yes, but it may wet your head' and laughed. Then when the practitioner probed further as to how she could carry the vessel so well, Nazia was able to say, 'I carry water every day for maaji (mother)' and 'I like doing it'. Sensitive dialogue enabled the practitioner to assess Nazia's previous experience and what her language proficiency was. The practitioner then planned to assess her learning in Literacy (DfE, 2012) based on these observations. Nazia was able to draw herself and write few words about her activity in English mixed with a few in her own native Urdu/Pashto language. The practitioner then shared this story with rest of the group. She asked other practitioners in the setting if they could also capture such stories/events to build a holistic picture of Nazia to share with others. This in turn showed Nazia's language competency, comprehension and construction.

Regular training for all practitioners on the needs of EAL learners

Continuous practitioner development is paramount to keep abreast of new developments and strategies. The needs of learners with EAL can be complex and require updated knowledge and understanding of issues of planning and assessment (see Chapter 4). However, we do realise that this may not be possible and offer an example of what one Early Years setting did to support practice. Located in a rural area, this setting has a history of having very few learners with EAL. However, over the past five years this pattern has changed following the arrival of new international migrants in the area. Ten per cent of their learners in the setting now have EAL and the majority of them are new arrivals – a trend which seems to be growing. This change in learner population has resulted in practitioners having to plan in a different way to accommodate the needs of these learners. One strategy they used was to twin the setting with a similar sized setting in an urban area which had an EAL learner population of 70 per cent. Practitioners took it in turns to visit this setting to observe and participate in aspects of planning and teaching. Over time practitioners began to work together between the two different settings to share training and resources to support each other to benefit all learners. The impact of this initiative was long lasting for the learners with EAL because they were more self-confident of their own identities. The practitioners also gained more knowledge about different teaching and learning strategies through sharing.

These brief examples demonstrate how practitioners in different Early Years settings have tried to meet Ofsted's (2012) key features of good practice, which has helped them to build a holistic picture of the individual learner. Continuing the support of learners with EAL requires sharing of next steps in learning with the learners in a way that is accessible and meaningful to them. Therefore practitioners need to be cautious about not mapping learners' next steps in a linear way, but should rather look for possible next steps. Good observations therefore lead to good monitoring and effective planning for possible next steps for learners. Much can be learned if we let go of our own ideas of how learners learn, and instead be an equal partner in the learning process. As Mistry and Sood (2011) found, many practitioners were unsure of how best to cater and plan for varied cultural needs of their learners. This requires an honest appraisal of a setting's own practitioner development needs and builds in specific programmes within the setting's development plan, mapped and monitored against successful criteria developed for a whole setting. Before we go into the specifics of planning, it is vital to mention the link between planning and assessment as both go hand in hand.

The link between planning and assessment

There is an integral link between planning and assessment in that one cannot happen without the other. Planning is often translated into practice as assessed as outcomes. Gripton (cited in Woods, 2013: 8) suggests that such an approach is very much a practitioner-centred way of planning and assessing. An alternative approach is to plan for possibilities, doing away with the shackles of and constraints of meeting specific Early Learning Goals. Such an approach is based on facilitating learning and the thesis that the learner, as an insider, is in control of their learning supported by the practitioner (ibid.). This debate may have merit, as we know planning requires an understanding of the context which enables learning. Planning is a complex activity as it needs an awareness of many different factors, indoor and outdoor learning, for example, as well as deep understanding of the nature of learning and the unique nature of childhood (ibid.: 9). Assessment forms an element of planning, where it is an integral process charting knowledge and understanding of learners' learning and development. It is an opportunity for practitioner reflection and action based on evidence collection. We develop the notion of assessment *of* learning, which is summative, and assessment *for* learning, which is an ongoing process for next step planning and provision.

Beginning planning for learners with EAL in practice

Planning differs from setting to setting because each context and learner cohort is different. In order to provide high quality in Early Years, planning and its associated learning through the activities planned have to be purposeful to encourage all learners to be confident and independent. In Table 5.1 we suggest what good planning should include and how this can be viewed in practice through examples for learners who have EAL.

The ideas in Table 5.1 can be used as a starting point for structuring planning for a setting. Most planning frameworks incorporate all these ideas for all learners in different ways. Next we go through the planning cycle and its adaptation for learners with EAL.

The planning cycle

Ofsted's (2012) framework requires monitoring attainment by ethnicity. To make sure all EAL learners in a setting are making progress, having them targeted through the planning cycle seems a sensible starting point. Although there are different approaches to planning, the common thread in all of them is to ensure that we have a 'clear overview of the learners' time in the setting' (Daly *et al.*, 2004: 80). Some settings will plan certain things in a similar way owing to constraints of the setting timetable, such as open days, festivals and special days, celebrations, community events and formal assessments.

Table 5.1 Good planning related to learners with EAL

Elements of good planning necessary for all learners	Examples for learners with EAL in Early Years
Find out what the learners already know and build on this	Use of resources and learner-initiated play to listen to any form of language and previous experience regardless of whether it is English or their home language.
Equal opportunities for all learners to promote inclusion	Not to be excluded from learning due to their language barrier; instead use songs and rhymes with actions to encourage participation.
Ensuring consistency and standards through each area of learning	If one area of learning is not covered in a given week, make this clear on planning to ensure it gains priority the following week; link to activities that reinforce key skills and language comprehension. Also highlight learning for EAL learners to show progression over time.
Encouraging all staff to be reflective in their practice	Ask practitioners to discreetly observe each other to identify one aspect of good practice in a week and then to share this in a team meeting, or via a staff good practice board. This can include type of questions used, resources used, adult intervention, peer support, translation support, use of parents.
Effective teamwork to ensure early interventions to avoid failure	Also ask staff to identify something they feel did not go so well with their EAL learner(s) over a week and the reason why. What support do staff and learners with EAL need?

In some ways these events provide a rhythm to the year – a pattern that is variable and flexible depending on contextual factors, but is also fairly predictable year on year – and therefore this can be described as long-term planning in terms of the events that need to be included in planning. Long-term plans in essence are the overview of the year and can be themed in terms of events, topics, skills, or a combination of all. Between long-term planning and the experiences that are planned for learners on a daily and weekly basis is medium-term plans that are made to ensure that over a term or half a term certain topics or themes are addressed through all areas of learning. In essence medium-term planning is not only the bridge between long- and short-term planning, but also the umbrella that ensures all areas are covered consistently over a period of time through a given theme.

All of these types of plans need to be in place so that all the necessary resources can be gathered. However, all planning should be flexible and used as a guide rather than followed slavishly. Although all aspects of planning are important, the most vital planning that is done is the short-term daily/weekly planning, because this incorporates discussions between the learners (and possibly their parents) and the practitioners, and is therefore based around their current interests and the EYFS (DfE, 2014). This short-term planning is more developmental and therefore should make it easier to track learners' progress. Links to a range of planning templates have been included later on in this chapter to give support.

In Figure 5.1 we have created a basic planning cycle to help with initial planning for learners with EAL, whereby the learner is at the heart of the process. In order to deconstruct this planning cycle, in Table 5.2 we have suggested some ideas to support each aspect of the cycle through specific things to reflect on for learners with EAL.

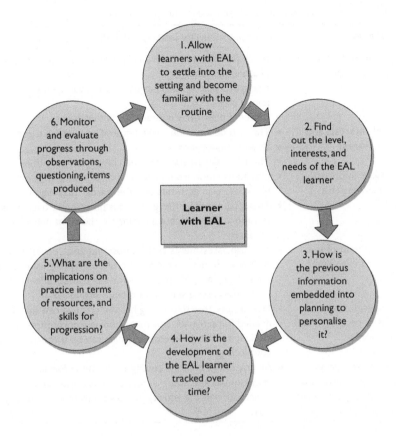

Figure 5.1 Basic planning cycle applicable to learners with EAL

Table 5.2 offers some generic ideas to be used as a starting point. However, these can be made more specific through a given theme. So, for example, if the theme is toys, then the resources may consist of a variety of toys with the associated language in terms of the movement of the toy, what it can be used for, how it can be changed, or how it encourages collaboration or builds skills with other learners.

Through this basic planning cycle we have incorporated what Ofsted (2012) identifies as key features of good planning. To embed good practice further, the planning cycle will benefit from practitioner reflection and self-analysis. This basically means that from this process the next steps for future learning need to be made clear by the practitioner. In addition we suggest the following ideas to support the planning process in practice:

- meeting EAL learners' needs, culture and interests sensitively through differentiation via observations and assessments;
- providing creative and challenging opportunities in all areas of learning with a balance of learner- and practitioner-initiated learning;
- allocating tasks in supporting practitioners so that they are fully involved; and
- identifying how current provision can be enhanced to provide enjoyable experiences for the future.

Table 5.2 Examples of aspects of a planning cycle utilised for learners with EAL

Aspect of the planning cycle	Possible application for learners with EAL
1 Allow learners with EAL to settle into the setting and become familiar with the routine	• Allow learners to observe what is going on (support silent phase if necessary) • Use gestures and body language to encourage them to join in play • Observe their early interactions with others
2 Find out the level, interests and needs of the EAL learner	• Through observations in structured and unstructured play • By asking questions • Though initial assessments and conversations with parents
3 How is the previous information embedded into planning to personalise it?	• Use information from previous practitioners or parents to initially plan activities that the learner may enjoy • Then plan to make these activities progressive over time to raise attainment, but allowing for the silent period if necessary
4 How is the development of the EAL learner tracked over time?	• Through assessments such as observations, conversations with practitioners in the setting, photographing aspects of the learning process (such as working collaboratively with others), assessing skills in outcomes produced
5 What are the implications for practice in terms of resources and skills for progression?	• Making sure that the setting has the creative resources needed for activities, and that planning incorporates challenge to aid progression (which can be through questioning)
6 Monitor and evaluate progress through observations, questioning, and end products (such as pictures, models, or examples of writing)	• All practitioners in the setting to do this in formal (assessment) and informal (quick mental note, or a quick intervention in the activity, or to go into role during play) ways

This is also supported by the notion in the EYFS that 'practitioners must consider the individual needs, interests, and stage of development of each child in their care, and must use this information to plan a challenging and enjoyable experience for each child in all areas of learning and development' (DfE, 2014).

There are many different planning formats and templates one can use in Early Years settings. As practitioners we will like some and dislike others as a result of our personal style of working. It is wise to collect as many different types of formats as possible and discuss which ones are most appropriate for learners with EAL. As we noted earlier, the templates are skeletal frameworks to be adapted in a given context.

A suggested planning framework for learners with EAL

South (1999: 17) has suggested stages of planning and delivery that are necessary when planning a sequence of lessons. We have adapted South's original framework to focus on learners with EAL. The left-hand column in Table 5.3 shows key skills which are necessary for all learners especially in relation to the prime areas in the EYFS (DfE, 2012), and the right-hand column shows our suggested adaptations for learners with EAL.

Table 5.3 Use of a planning framework for learners with EAL

Consideration for all learners in Early Years	Key points for practitioners	Suggestions for learners with EAL in Early Years
• Finding out the starting point of learners' previous experience within the EYFS and the associated skills, knowledge and understanding • Current level of Communication and Language in association with the other prime areas • Setting environment and its impact on class/group organisation	Planning knowledge, understanding and skills	• Varying level of spoken language, focus on key words with visual cues • Impact of previous experiences through play and prior educational experience • Identification and use of home language • Identification and impact of home culture (which is different in each household)
• Looking at the content of the areas of learning in the EYFS and linking objectives progressively to the theme of the term	Developing knowledge, understanding and skills	• Prior experience is essential in order to match curriculum knowledge and understanding, associated language, structure, genres
• Creative teaching associated with the needs of the learners to promote talk and learning connections through modelling, ICT, play, questioning to aid comprehension, etc.	Teaching	• Adapting creative teaching to encompass visual cues, model activity and role play, mixed groupings for peer observations and promotion of talk, use of songs and ICT to encourage repetition
• Activities that reinforce developmental knowledge, understanding and skills in each area of learning linked to a theme – both indoors and outdoors	Adult- and learner-initiated learning activities	• Adjustments of spoken language and activity expectations in terms of different outcomes; practical activities to encourage engagement with peers through the use of indoor and outdoor resources
• Assessing outcomes through questioning, models, show and tell, games, role play	Assessment and next steps for learning	• Assessing outcomes through key language words, questioning using modelling and visual cues, using peers to collaborate on feedback, and show and tell to promote talk and group work

The distinctiveness of planning in Early Years comes not only from the type of learning strategies, but also from the breadth of creative strategies that practitioners need to draw on. In Figure 5.2 we suggest a basic planning template that can be used as an initial starting point.

Lesson planning sheet	Early Years
Date:	Time: Group: (including target learners)
Area of learning: Learning intention:	
Link to prior learning (context)	
Key vocabulary:	Key questions:
Introduction (including differentiation)	
Main activity (including differentiation)	
Supporting activities (including differentiation) and outdoor learning	
Plenary (including differentiation)	
Role of supporting adults	
Use of resources	
Opportunities for assessment (in addition to observation)	
Next steps for learning	
Evaluation to inform future planning	

Figure 5.2 Blank template for planning

Our suggested planning template is a very basic one that should be adapted to suit the context and setting. It is wise to have a medium-term planning grid or plan that this lesson planning template builds on in order to ensure that all areas of learning are addressed over a period of time. In Figure 5.3 this same lesson planning template has been completed for learners with EAL with suggested examples to support initial guidance regarding a planning structure for a given area of learning (Understanding the World; DfE, 2012).

Lesson planning sheet	Early Years
Date: (such as day and month)	**Time:** (length of time for the activity – approximately 20 mins) **Group:** (including target learners)
Area of learning: Understanding the World **Learning intention:** To identify who lives in my home	
Link to prior learning (context) (What do learners with EAL already know or remember from their prior learning? Context has to be engaging and motivating) Linked to the theme of 'Ourselves', have had a prior discussion of people such as mum and dad through photos	
Key vocabulary: Teach specific key language (questions to focus on key language/specific words and their comprehension in or contextual words) **Key questions:** Such as: Who lives at home with you? (mum/dad/brother/sister/pet) Do you know where other people in your family live? (which may be in the home language – through a translator)	
Introduction (including differentiation) (Introductory activity with visual resources (pictures/puppets/music/interactive whiteboard to show video clips) to engage learner's interest, or if possible through the use of a translator to support the process) Differentiation can be through the use of a supporting practitioner or through different questions. Clarification of the learning intention. Possibly begin with who lives in the practitioner's home through photos	
Main activity (including differentiation) A selection of activities to support the learning intention. Activities are differentiated with practitioner support, and key questions to ascertain learner's comprehension. • Use photographs to help learners with EAL identify the people and pets that live with them – how do they refer to older or younger siblings (some cultures may not use the first name of people but a term such as bhai – meaning brother) • Discussion on what is the role of the people they live with (who goes to work where)	

Figure 5.3 An example of a completed planning template

Supporting activities (including differentiation) and outdoor learning

(A selection of activities to support the learning intention through learner initiated activities, including outdoor learning. Activities are differentiated with practitioner support, and key questions take place intermittently through practitioner intervention)

- Use a dolls house and small world to support role play
- Use a dressing up area to observe what the roles of different family members are; including a variety of clothing worn
- Drawing pictures/painting people in the home
- Use outdoor area to set up as a kitchen and lounge to see how learners model the people in their home through play

Photographs could also be taken as you observe learners in their roles for discussion in the plenary.

Plenary (including differentiation)

Re-cap on introduction and learning intention through associated activities. Maybe a show and tell session to see how well learners with EAL have responded and contributed.

Bring group together to discuss what they have been learning through their chosen or directed activity. Use photos taken to help stimulate discussion if necessary

Role of supporting practitioners

Roles and responsibilities of supporting practitioners – whether this is observing, or asking key questions, or being involved in role play

Use of resources

Resources selected to support this lesson and how they are adapted for learners with EAL

Opportunities for assessment (in addition to observation)

Continuous assessment including photographs, making notes, formal/informal observations
Having knowledge of an EAL learner's current targets

Next steps for learning

What went well and why, and what was the impact of this on learning?
What did not go so well and why, and what was the impact of this on learning?
What surprised you from the observations and questioning that took place and why?

Evaluation to inform future planning

How can it be identified that learners with EAL have made progress?
How can you ensure the transference of skills gained by learners with EAL?
How can the learning intention be extended in different contexts?

Figure 5.3 (continued)

It is paramount for the setting to find a planning template that works for all to aid consistency. As previously mentioned, what works in one setting may not work in another, and therefore planning templates will change with time and government directives.

Challenges of planning in Early Years

The biggest challenge regarding planning in Early Years is that there is no set format or guidance for the way in which this should be carried out, especially for learners with EAL. Each setting will have their own formats dependant on their context and the needs of their learners. From our experience, Table 5.4 shows some challenges faced by practitioners regarding planning.

Some strategies to support these challenges have been offered, but we are mindful that there are many more challenges associated with planning for our learners with EAL

Table 5.4 Challenges of planning in Early Years

Challenge regarding planning	Possible strategies for learners with EAL	Suggested examples
What happens to those learners who do not achieve the ELGs by the end of the reception year?	There needs to be a different kind of transition between Early Years and Key Stage One in the sense that working towards the ELGs may need to continue for a short period of time in a Year 1 class so that learners settle in a new environment quickly. Assessments will also need to reflect this personalised approach.	Having more play-based activities in Y1 initially to keep aspects of the previous environment familiar. Also using observations to assess learning for learners with EAL in different subjects before the more formal assessments take over.
Differentiating learning in planning that may not always work	Keep planning flexible and allow the learning journey to be taken in different directions especially though language comprehension and vocabulary. Critically reflect on the learning that has taken place rather than the original outcome not achieved.	Using critical evaluations and experience in planning to change activities if they do not seem to work. Make assessments on the process (or conversations) that learners with EAL go through during activities rather than the expected end outcome.
How assessment feeds into planning to ensure progress for learners with EAL	If language is a barrier for EAL learners in your setting, then your assessment may be in smaller steps. Assessments may also have to be adjusted to include key words in the home language to show progression, or to be carried out with the aid of a translator, or as a collaborative group task.	Focus on key terminology which is repeated for learners with EAL in activities and use questioning to assess comprehension.
When planning is based on previous experience of working with EAL learners	We need to remember that previous experience of EAL learners is a good starting point, but every learner is unique and therefore we need to build positive relationships so that we know our learners well. In this way, we are aware that what works for one EAL learner, may not work for another.	Intervene in play or observe play to get to know learners with EAL better so that this knowledge can be used to help personalise planning as much as possible.

dependent on the experience(s) of the practitioner. In the majority of cases, issues with planning can be associated with a lack of confidence in working with such diverse learners who may not show any progress for a while (silent phase).

Summary

This chapter considered some of the processes needed for planning in the Early Years. If we accept the notion that a learner is an active and creative actor in their learning, then we need to understand that practitioners must continue to set aside space and time for themselves to plan flexibly so as to build on a learner's own interest. As Woods (2013: preface) says, we need planning that takes account of the unexpected rather than relying on templates which can be the case for learners with EAL. According to the EYFS (DfE, 2014), there are many opportunities for inclusive practice that necessitate organisation and planning of indoor and outdoor learning environments. We offered a range of examples of planning for learners with EAL, suggesting that, as for all learners, their specific cultural and linguistic needs should be considered in planning. Creative and enjoyable learning requires creative planning where the practitioner plans with a mind open to all possibilities and this means a can-do culture where different ways of working and planning in collaboration with other practitioners and working with parents and outside agencies is fostered.

Useful links to support planning in Early Years

We offer a number of possible models of planning to offer a starting point in different contexts that can be adapted by Early Years settings. As practitioners we need to look out for all possibilities for planning, from those involving the learner at the centre stage and to endless possibilities based on future thinking. The creativity of practitioners allows for modelling, reflecting and evaluating practice to explore what is possible for learners in a given context. As the contexts of our settings change to accommodate a more diverse population, settings need to take further practical steps to plan 'for limitless learning' (Gripton, cited in Woods, 2013: 18) based on the cultural values, beliefs and customs of their varied learner population. Rather than having a chapter full of planning templates, we suggest here a number of useful planning formats and guidance in Early Years that may be useful in supporting the planning process. Many of these are from various county councils in England that have a diverse EAL learner population, and are used as a starting point for settings. The web links were accessed in April 2014.

> Examples of blank planning templates:
> www.wiltshire.gov.uk/eyfs-planning-examples-pack.pdf
>
> EYFS: Good practice guidelines:
> www.childrenscentres.org.uk/EYFS_Good_Practice_Guidelines.asp
>
> Planning sheets for individual learners:
> www.surreycc.gov.uk/learning/early-years-and-childcare-service/early-years-practitioners-and-providers/early-years-foundation-stage-paperwork#Templates
>
> Planning guidelines and templates:
> www.childrenscentres.org.uk/ey_planning.asp

Range of planning sheets from 0 to 5 years:
www.yor-ok.org.uk/Workforce/Working%20with%20Children,%20Young%20
People%20and%20Families/Early%20Years%20and%20Childrens%20Centres/
revised-eyfs-observation-assessment-and-planning.htm

Tracking sheets for EYFS:
http://education.staffordshire.gov.uk/Curriculum/Strategies/EarlyYears/
learning-and-development/observation/

Weekly Early Years planning guide and examples:
www.islington.gov.uk/services/children-families/cs-about-childrens-services/early_
years/foundation_stage/planning_for_children/Pages/short_term_planning.aspx

---

Reflective questions

- Now you know how to start planning, within your team, develop one planning sheet for your learners with EAL.
- Describe within your plan one or two learning points that must be included for learners with EAL. This chapter suggests that planning needs to be adjusted in light of the group or context. So what opportunities can be provided through planning for learners with EAL to work in different ways with their peers?
- How is planning made consistently progressive regarding EAL learners' development in a setting?

References

Daly, M., Byres, E. and Taylor, W. (2004) *Early Years: management in practice*. Oxford: Heinemann.

Department for Education (DfE) (2012) *Statutory framework for the Early Years Foundation Stage (EYFS)*. London: DfE.

Department for Education (DfE) (2014) *Statutory framework for the Early Years Foundation Stage (EYFS)*. London: DfE, https://www.gov.uk/government/uploads/system/uploads/attachment_data/file/299391/DFE-00337-2014.pdf (accessed April 2014).

Drake, J. (2010) *Planning for children's play and learning*. 3rd edn. London: Routledge.

Farmer, G. (2002) Dolls with stories to tell: understanding bias and diversity, in C. Nutbrown (ed.), *Research studies in early childhood education*. Stoke-on-Trent: Trentham Books, pp. 141–57.

Fisher, R. (1996) *Stories for thinking*. Oxford: Nash Pollock.

Gaine, C. (1995) *Still no problem here*. Stoke-on-Trent: Trentham Books.

Hopkins, D. (1994) *Evaluation for school development*. Milton Keynes: Open University Press.

Mistry, M. and Sood, K. (2011) Raising standards for pupils who have English as Additional Language (EAL) through monitoring and evaluation of provision in primary schools, www.tandfonline.com/loi/rett20 (accessed March 2014).

Moss, P. and Petrie, P. (2002) *From children's services to children's spaces: public policy, children and childhood*. London: RoutledgeFalmer.

National Association for Language Development in the Curriculum (NALDIC) (2012) *EYFS and EAL: supporting bilingual children in the Early Years*, www.naldic.org.uk/eal-teaching-and-learning/outline-guidance/early-years (accessed April 2014).

Office for Standards in Education (Ofsted) (2009) Twenty outstanding primary schools – excelling against the odds, ref. 090170, www.ofsted.gov.uk/resources/twenty-outstanding-primary-schools-excelling-against-odds (accessed November 2014).

Office for Standards in Education (Ofsted) (2010) *Inspecting equalities – guidance for section 5 inspectors*, ref. 090197, www.flse.org.uk/documents/Equalities_Guidance%20for%20inspectors_Sept%202009%20(Ofsted)-rDQkjyw0YvazRCTI-1264419046.pdf (accessed November 2014).

Office for Standards in Education (Ofsted) (2012) *The evaluation schedule for the inspection of maintained schools and academies January 2012*, ref. 090098. London: Ofsted.

South, H. (ed.) (1999) *The distinctiveness of English as an Additional Language: a cross-curricular discipline.* Watford: NALDIC.

Taguchi, H. L. (2010) *Going beyond the theory/practice divide in early childhood education: introducing an intra-active pedagogy.* London: Routledge.

Unique teaching resources (2014) 600 quotes about education and learning, www.uniqueteachingresources.com/Quotes-About-Education.html (accessed May 2014).

Woods, A. (ed.) (2013) *Child-initiated play and learning.* London: Routledge.

Chapter 6

The pedagogy of play for learners with EAL

'Through play at school I could hear the leaves rustle and go on a journey.'
Adapted from Clint Eastwood (Khurana, 2014)

The aims of this chapter

- To conceptualise the term 'play' for learners with EAL
- To explore the role of the practitioner in supporting play for learning for learners with EAL
- To develop knowledge and understanding of the pedagogy of play within the context for learners with EAL

Overview

In this chapter, we look at the notion of play, its multiple definitions with its link to pedagogy, its link to theory of learning and its utility for those learners who have EAL. We begin by looking at what play is from theory and our own experiences. For some EAL learners, the notion of play can be a bewildering experience, especially if they do not fully understand the language used by some practitioners. Next we look at some theories associated with play linked to learning and teaching approaches. We use research findings and observations of various Early Years settings to see how the role and value of play amongst different learners with EAL are promoted. We then consider how an EAL learner and practitioner work together to support play through, for example, observing, interacting, and providing for development, engagement and enrichment to promote learning. Finally, this chapter considers a number of practical strategies offered for reflection and some perspectives on developing play in monocultural/monolingual settings to help support practice, especially for isolated learners with EAL.

Key words: observing play, making connections, exploration, co-collaboration, monolingual

Introduction

The idea of play is unique compared with other forms of human activity owing to its qualities of natural spontaneity, creativity, and whether it is self- or practitioner-initiated.

Across the many different cultures in society, it is human nature to like to play. This is because play enables learners to explore the customs, traditions and roles of their lifestyle and community; to reflect upon their inner selves and their emotions; to encounter abstract thinking; and to develop communication skills without looking to achieve an end product. Play is also a universal concept that is inclusive and gender and age neutral. But because learners with EAL are 'not a homogenous group as there are possible variations between individuals and groups of EAL learners' (Ofsted, 2012: 3), we need to be mindful of the variations as these learners may come from diverse linguistic, cultural and educational backgrounds and therefore may have a different understanding of play in an educational context.

One reason for these different understandings may be differing levels of English language acquisition for these learners. Because play offers a unique opportunity for learners with EAL to acquire English in real-life situations where they start to understand 'the rules of English gradually' (EMTRAS, 2011: 5), collaboration with practitioners is helpful. For example, in role play learners can mimic each other regarding words used and rules of the English language in terms of pronunciation and meaning. What play offers is a chance to develop high cognitive challenges through rich language content which could be done by building support strategies and scaffolding learning through using games, pair talk, drama/role play areas, photographs, picture prompts, construction toys, guided reading, writing and artefacts. However, there are many definitions of play; next we try to deconstruct the term before offering our own definition.

What is play?

Play is one of the most important ways of learning and developing for all young learners regardless of their background or the context. It is also an activity that is viewed as being fun and can take place in different formats, such as through games, structured play, free play and role play, both indoors and outdoors. Play is a vital way of supporting all aspects of learning, but especially the personal, social and emotional development of learners in order to give them the skills to be able to socialise with others. Bruner (1983: 43, quoted in Bruce 1997: 31) describes free play or learner-initiated play as 'preparation for the technical and social life that constitutes human culture'. Similarly, Montessori (1912) placed importance on learners learning about reality. She viewed pretend play as primitive and felt that learners benefit from practitioner guidance to enable them to explore the properties of the real world through specially constructed didactic play materials.

Play can include the symbolic use of objects. It offers learners an opportunity to pretend and try out role play without the boundaries of rules, which is especially important for learners with EAL. Play is, in fact, more often than not, fun, and does not have to have an end outcome. More importantly, play is how learners make connections between their inner and outer worlds (Wood and Attfield, 2006: 4) and is very much learner-invented as described in Meckley's (2002, cited in Wood and Attfield, 2006: 4–5) framework. So 'play with' and 'play at' (Wood and Attfield, 2006: 5) are helpful starting concepts to consider when we try to make sense of the notion of play, as it is culturally, socially and environmentally/context bound.

Different cultural backgrounds and contexts can interpret play in multiple ways. For example, some learners with EAL who are new arrivals from China may find play in Early Years settings in England a new concept, which could be a result of being familiar with a different, more formal kind of education system that does not include play. Alternatively, for example, some learners with EAL from countries like Finland may find the formal side of learning in Early Years in England a new concept as they do not start formal education until the age of six or seven, with a heavy focus of learning through play as shown in Case study 6.1.

Case study 6.1

Leena is a five-year-old female and a new EAL arrival in a reception setting from Finland. The home visit showed that although she was familiar and confident with family in the home environment in terms of conversation and play, she was shy in front of all new people. After she started in her reception setting, it was noticed that she was happy to work with her peers in free choice and play activities regardless of her lack of English language acquisition. However, she would stand back and watch when more formal group learning directed by a practitioner took place. This was especially evident in literacy- and numeracy-based activities, where she did not have the language understanding to know what was expected of her.

Case study 6.1 shows that because play is considered to be a universal activity, learners from different cultural backgrounds and different contexts will interpret play in multiple ways regardless of whether they fully understand the spoken language or not. However, as the case study highlights, this may not be the same for the more specific aspects of the Early Years Foundations Stage (EYFS). This means that care has to be taken at the planning stage to better integrate learners with EAL with the indigenous learner group. Reed and Canning (2010) suggest that defining play depends on how play is seen and in what context: as an object (what is play?) or as an act (what happens in play in terms of creating meaning?) which is explored next.

Defining play through theory

Play is defined and understood in many different ways, a cultural perspective being just one approach. The concept is full of questions and dilemmas faced by practitioners (Wood and Attfield, 2006: vii) regarding the role and value of play in learning. Early theories of play such as those presented by Rousseau (1712–78), Pestalozzi (1746–1827) and Froebel (1782–1852) (cited in Johnston and Nomad-Williams, 2009) tended to concentrate on the physical features of play such as the importance of gross motor skills and physical development (EYFS) (DfE, 2014). Later theorists such as Dewey (1859–1952), Montessori (1870–1952), Steiner (1861–1925), Piaget (1896–1980) and Vygotsky (1896–1934) (cited in Johnston and Nomad-Williams, 2009) focused mainly on the internal, emotional functions of play such as the social side of play and collaboration (Personal, Social and Emotional Development, EYFS) (DfE, 2014). The cognitive role of play (the link to learning) became more prominent in the mid-twentieth century, and has been a key feature of later approaches to play, thus influencing the development of services for young learners. More recently, theories associated with play (see below) view it as a holistic activity, for learner development within a social context.

The significance of play within the developmental context of Early Years has been increasingly recognised and valued, particularly by those who work in the sector. However, the relevance of play as a tool for learning needs greater clarity for many practitioners and parents outside Early Years. Today, from a developmental perspective, we draw on a rich range of theories, enabling us to value play as a vital aspect of the learning that takes place in the Early Years (DfE, 2014), which is vital for learners with additional needs including learners with EAL. One thought that needs to be considered is the understanding of how parents of learners with EAL can view play, where perhaps for some, play may not be viewed as a natural form of learning. For example, some parents of learners with EAL may not be clear about the role of play in the EYFS, and therefore can be slightly confused when they come into a setting and see opportunities for play set up. So what is needed is a newly conceptualised, or rather, re-conceptualised notion of play based on theory and practice. This means that there is no one single definition of play that will satisfy all audiences, which is why it can remain a contentious issue and we hope that a setting can come to their own working definition within individual contexts.

We therefore define play as any activity which promotes learning through active involvement either alone or with others. It can happen anywhere, at any time and in any circumstance or context. The notion of play can be learner-generated or practitioner-generated. It can be imaginative, fun, collaborative or not and highly motivating for the individual. It may involve self-selection of resources or not. The process of play has no beginning or ending as it is sometimes self-directed (with the practitioner in an observer role perhaps) by the learner leading to much incidental learning like co-operative or problem-solving skills. Let us briefly turn to what some theorists say about play.

Play and EAL

Developing language may be one key aspect of learning through play for learners with EAL; another is developing social and interactive skills through the use of resources. Behaviourist researchers like Skinner (1953) conceptualise play as a learnt response to a set of stimuli – for example, toys. Play is seen as a set of problem-solving behaviours, for both learners with EAL and those without, because of its complex and investigative features. For some these features of play are a means of developing skills, such as co-operation, collaboration, risk taking and communication, and more importantly their imagination of real and unreal scenarios. For learners with EAL play also has the added emphasis of developing communication skills to support English language acquisition. Such learners also mimic their own cultural upbringing through role play or imaginative play, using stories they may have heard from their families or, more often now, watching cultural/ceremonial events and intercultural movies. In our experience, we have seen that learners without EAL will often talk about what a character will say and do, and then go on, in character, to act this out, but this may not be as evident for learners with EAL, especially if their life experiences to date have been different.

This ability to reflect on communication, as Bateson (1983) observes, provides learners with meta-communication skills – that is, the ability to reflect upon and consider the functions and forms of communication. Piaget (1962) moved the focus on play away from social and emotional development and towards cognitive development.

He argued that play contributes to intellectual development through the processes of accommodation and assimilation. We consider assimilation to be the dominant mode in play, where learners achieve through play by taking an idea and making it fit with what they already know and understand. For learners with EAL, this means that they are free to learn through play without necessarily having to know the language needed to explore and interact in play activity. Language of course is important, but is there an opportunity for practitioners to listen, observe and make note of what language the learner with EAL might be using? What this may say about the setting is that it allows for the use of different languages by the learners which is celebrated and encouraged.

The theory of Vygotsky (1962) emphasised (like other theorists in this chapter) that play is the leading activity of childhood, as it supports all aspects of a learner's development. Added to this, Vygotsky went on to highlight the importance of social and cultural factors in the development of play. He noted that make-believe play is socially and culturally determined, and as learners explore this type of play, they are deepening their understanding of the social life and rules of their communities. We next consider the multifaceted role of the learner in play, which is dependent on the context of the setting.

Role of the learner in play

There are many roles of learners in play: learners as on-lookers; solitary play as a learner plays alone; parallel play, when learners play alongside but not with each other; and group play, when learners play together. This makes it even harder for practitioners to follow, understand and encapsulate learners' imaginative free play. Practitioners, by their very presence, will affect learners' play and the introduction of film and video as research tools has provided an additional dimension of investigation into play. Most learners have their own mental schemas/road maps of how they play either alone or with peers, for example with using resources such as play dough as a stimulus provided by the practitioner. For learners with EAL, they may need time to observe other peers in play before they have the confidence to join in. This is because expectations in play are not always as clear as they are in other, more formal activities; thus practitioners need to continue to allow learners with EAL to problem-solve at their own pace through supportive and enabling teaching which is further explored next.

Role of the practitioner in play

With greater emphasis now on accountability within the White Paper (DfE, 2010), there is an increasing expectation that practitioners will have a greater role in planning, supporting and extending learner's learning by developing the pedagogy of play. Promoting access and inclusion is high on the British government's agenda for learners with additional needs, but promotion of such a policy to include learners with EAL appears to be somewhat lacking. We suggest that a setting undertakes its own analysis to tease out what constitutes play and what cultural issues should be addressed as these are unique to each setting. In considering the strategies for play with learners with EAL, resources aid the development of learning though first-hand play. For example, the use of toys and role play can assist with the development of visual, auditory and kinaesthetic abilities as the learners engage and interact with the different stimuli. Labelling resources verbally and or pictorially develops in the learners the value and importance of writing at their own level. Using multicultural resources adds further interest, and there has been some rather dated research which has shown that learners as young as four recognise and put a value to colour.

Practical ways to develop play for learners with EAL

We know that one of the best ways of learning for Early Years learners is in a social context linked to real-life opportunities and experiences. Play is often said to provide a vehicle for learners to create meaning from their experiences (Bruce 1997). In addition it also offers an opportunity for socialisation and interaction allowing for rich language learning from others and through good role models. Below are some ideas to support practice, particularly for learners with EAL.

- Take a little time to observe, find out what the learners with EAL like playing and why, and what are their roles and intentions. Consider whether practitioners need to intervene in play, and for what purposes (such as offering suggestions, introducing new ideas or vocabulary, managing the noise or behaviour, extending the activity through additional resources or negotiating entry for another learner).
- Try to play on the learners' terms by taking on a role that they suggest, and following their instructions. With the youngest learners, participating alongside and imitating a learner's actions with the same type of materials will often signal that practitioners are in tune and start a playful interaction. Offer some ideas when certain that they are consistent with the flow of the play.
- Avoid going into closed questioning ('How many? What colour? What size?'). Instead, try to maintain playful ways of engaging by following learners' directions and tuning into their meanings.
- Try not to direct the play to the learning objectives or assessment agenda.
- Try to be alert to the qualities of play, and to the knowledge and skills that learners are using and applying (DCSF, 2009).

Practitioners have an important role therefore during play activity in extending the learners' support of English if they are learners with EAL (NALDIC, 2012). However, we need more research and practice-based evidence to see how the role and value of play amongst learners with EAL is promoted through cultural introduction. It is already well noted that play is a central feature of learning and development in the Early Years. Therefore next we link play to the EYFS.

Play and the EYFS

Play is central to the way in which the curriculum is shaped and delivered in England using the Early Years Foundation Stage (EYFS) statutory guidance (DfE, 2014). The authors undertook observations of learners with EAL in reception settings where there was a high percentage (70 per cent and above) of learners with EAL, to find out how play promoted their cognitive development. We used Piaget's (1962) three categories and stages of play – practice play (mainly exploratory type of play); symbolic play (pretend and fantasy) and games with rules; and constructive play (Smilansky, 1990) – to develop our understanding. We found that learners needed to be given wider opportunities than currently available to play both indoors and outdoors. This could be through structured and unstructured means so that the learners with EAL could make their own choices and decisions as well as mistakes through risk taking. By creating these opportunities through play, we concluded that learners could observe, mimic and collaborate with one another. These we believe are the skills that are so vital for the prime areas of learning. These skills may also support the academic learning that takes place through the areas of learning in the EYFS. Next we offer some examples of play we observed being used for learners with EAL linked to each area of learning within the EYFS that could help support practice.

Example 1: Prime area – Communication and Language

Leela was an only child. Although her parents were fluent in English, they had made a decision to focus on the home language at home and therefore Leela came to her reception class not being able to speak any English at all. Her practitioners allowed Leela time to observe other learners in the setting and did not force her to carry out certain tasks on a one-to-one basis. Instead, they allowed her to interact with as many learners as possible through play. When feeding back to the parents, the practitioners discovered that the play observed during the day was carried out with her toys at home in English. Therefore Leela was observing in the setting and re-enacting her day at home. This example shows that it could be so useful to capture play experiences as a diary video to aid discussion amongst practitioners to further improve pedagogical practice for communication and language.

Example 2: Prime area – Physical Development

Sanjay was a very active four-year-old from a Swedish background. Although he was a learner with EAL, he understood basic words and instructions in English. His parents often used to tell the practitioner that he was a handful at home. He had a very low concentration span when it came to any table-based mark-making activity. However, when outside, he would suddenly become more focused, and seemed to enjoy this part of the setting most. Sanjay would spend a long time on the apparatus in the outdoor area as well as on the trikes and cars. He also enjoyed any physical activity. The practitioners in the reception setting set up an outdoor mark-making area which started to create some motivation for Sanjay to begin writing. This example shows that by trying to offer as many combined physical play-based learning opportunities as possible, practitioners can help learners with EAL develop the confidence to communicate in English.

Example 3: Prime area – Personal, Social and Emotional Development

Anil was from an Indo-Australian background. He was a quiet boy and had an older sister, which meant he was used to hearing English at home and was familiar with many words even though English was not the home language. However, he was reluctant to join in with the other learners in play activities, especially outdoor play. He would be happy to play on his own, but he found the company of many learners frightening initially. At playtime, he would look for his sister and play with her, but not with the other learners. The practitioners in the reception class then allowed Anil's sister to come into the reception setting at certain times during a setting week to encourage him to play with other learners and begin to engage socially. Towards the end of the year, although Anil was still quiet in comparison with other learners in the class, his spoken language had developed sufficiently for him to feel comfortable in playful learning in small groups. What this example shows is the need to continue to liaise more closely with the family to better bridge the communication gap through play-based learning, allowing Anil to feel more confident to join in with his peers and thus supporting his personal development.

Example 4: Specific area – Literacy

Junhua is from a Chinese background and the family only arrived in England two years ago. Within this time, Junhua has picked up the basics of the English language in terms of his speech as he has two older siblings who are more fluent. However, it is a very different story when it comes to reading and writing. Letters in the English alphabet are very different to Chinese characters, where sometimes one symbol means a phrase rather than just a sound. Therefore Junhua would avoid any activity in play that involved mark-making. The reception practitioners realised that they would have to try alternative strategies to encourage Junhua with his phonics and writing, so they used play dough, sand trays and large highlighter markers to encourage letter formation. They also used an iPad to encourage writing in a more fun context. Over time Junhua recognised his sounds, and began the basics of decoding for early reading. But it became apparent that his comprehension of text and phrases was very limited. This example shows how the learning environment to support play can be changed to encourage skills in literacy through language development in a fun and exciting way to support an EAL learner.

Example 5: Specific area – Understanding the World

Christopher was a new arrival in the reception setting from Gambia. He really enjoyed learning through the use of construction toys. Although his spoken English language was limited, he was able to identify key items made from mega blocks such as car, bus, boat. He knew what an aeroplane was as he remembered coming to England in one a few months earlier. When given free choice, Christopher always went to the construction area or the outdoor area; he found play in the role play area or play which involved practitioner intervention very difficult. After conversations with his mum, it emerged that this was Christopher's first educational experience. In Gambia, he was used to spending a lot of time outdoors, especially with boats as his uncle used to catch fish using his boat on a daily basis, and sometimes Christopher went with him. This example shows that learners with EAL are giving us hidden messages through their play. In the case of Christopher, he was linking his previous experience of the outdoor environment to construction toys.

Example 6: Specific area – Mathematics

Luisa was from Peru, and her first language was Spanish. She had some understanding of key words in English on arrival into the reception setting because she had two older siblings and therefore felt confident in mixing the home language and English. Her particular strength was in the area of number bonds in maths, especially with addition. She could mentally count to thirty and identify numbers in and out of order. She could do a variety of sums that included both addition and subtraction to thirty with the use of counting aids such as cubes and compare bears in any play context. However, she used to become very frustrated with her number formation in the written format, hence feeling somewhat dejected at times. This example shows that Luisa, like many learners with EAL, finds Mathematics easier than Literacy because of the similarities between numbers and number symbols in different languages. For example, the symbol for addition and numbers are the same in many languages.

Example 7: Specific area – Expressive Arts and Design

On arrival into the nursery setting Antonella, who was from an Italian background, spent a large part of her time using her fine motor skills to feel different materials such as play dough, sand, cornflour goo, water and sawdust rather than engaging in playful conversations. By the end of the year Antonella's familiarity with the nursery resources such as the multicultural clothes and accessories in the dressing up area gave her confidence to begin to engage in playful learning. The practitioners at the setting began to model how resources should be used in order to support Antonella during her play. This example shows that as practitioners, we need to offer as much variety of resources and experiences as possible, such as watching plays, making and using puppets, artwork, and experimenting with different materials that are safe, to motivate, engage and enthuse all learners, but especially those with EAL in a play context. As practitioners we need to find that magic moment that captures the excitement of learning which is easier through this area of learning.

These examples may appear to be stereotypical examples on the surface, but they demonstrate learners' lived experience as these EAL learners have reflected on the rituals they have seen in their social and cultural worlds. In our examples, not all stages of Piagetian theory were witnessed as learners developed their own paths to learning, adjusting their internal schema, discovering, exploring from learner-centred view of learning. The practitioner was the enabler and facilitator, questioning, supporting and scaffolding the learner's own meaning-making and learning. These play examples illustrate that learners need quality experiences in order to help them in their adult life. This begins in Early Years through play where they develop various skills, from social to academic through interactions with each other to support learning. This is especially the case for learners of EAL, and particularly those who are new arrivals, as their life context and experiences may be very different to those of the rest of their classmates.

Role of the parent in supporting play

Parents are crucial in supporting their learners with play because they are the first role models for learners with the greatest initial influence. It is well known that the support of parents has a huge impact on learners' achievement and development. This is particularly vital with parents of learners with EAL as their personal experiences of education may be very different to the way learning in Early Years is structured in England (through play).

Practitioners need to highlight that learners with EAL need to have an attempt at using English and even periods of silence (EMTRAS, 2011) in their play. Therefore we suggest that parents are offered strategies on play, or at least, encouraged to try things out with their learners to give them the concrete experience to develop linguistic skills and concepts. Such continuity between home and setting may 'aid confidence in communication and boost self-esteem' (EMTRAS, 2011: 7) as we show through Case study 6.2.

Case study 6.2

Ram has just started at the local reception setting. He is five years old and an only child. After her maternity leave was over, his mum chose to stay at home and be with him so that he would not have to go to a child minder. His mum believed that the best possible person to bring him up in the Early Years was herself, and therefore they were close and had a good relationship. Ram was happy to play with other learners as long as his mum played too and was happy to do most things with other learners if he had his mum with him. However, he did not go to other practitioners in the reception setting and would always try to hide behind his mum. His mum told the setting that he behaved like this at home as well and would not go near extended family members or family friends. The practitioners at the setting then gave Ram's mum suggestions of simple games which they could start off together initially (such as using construction toys) and then encourage other learners to join in, before she slowly starts to move away as Ram gains confidence in playing with others.

Case study 6.2 shows the importance of understanding one another's expectations and any concerns arising between home and setting, which it is helpful to sort out at the earliest opportunity so as to best meet the needs of the learner. However, there are also a number of challenges associated with play to which we turn next.

Potential challenges of play

Play is often tempered by constraints such as curriculum overload, top-down pressure from management, lack of resources and confusion around the contestable nature of play among those who do not appreciate its value. An interesting finding by NALDIC (2012) suggests that practitioners seem to remain distant from their EAL learners in play and it is vital that all practitioners try to close this emotional and conceptual distance by continuing to give these learners more praise and encouragement.

Our visits to Early Years settings and our discussions with practitioners have indicated various challenges with EAL learners in play as shown in Table 6.1.

The implications of the examples suggested in Table 6.1 are that practitioners need to be given time or find time to share their ideas of practice through discussions with individuals and teams. Some of the examples demonstrate that adequate resources or opportunities for play exist and practitioners deploy resources to maximise learning and

Table 6.1 Examples of how to meet some challenges of play with learners with EAL

Challenge regarding play	Possible strategies for learners with EAL	Suggested examples
Not knowing what the starting point is in play	Use observations and conversations as a starting point in play without an assessment focus initially	Anna, the practitioner, went into a role play in the home corner with Pooja and Chen and carefully encouraged both in playful conversations through open-ended, enabling dialogue.
Not knowing if learners with EAL are familiar with some of the resources we use	Put a range of familiar Early Years resources out (such as play dough, paints, sand/water trays, building blocks, etc.) and observe whether they are used by learners with EAL and how (whether they try on their own or copy how others use them)	Meera, a bilingual practitioner, worked with small groups for the first hour on play activities to model how resources should be used.
Sometimes when practitioners intervene in play, learners who are EAL become silent and stand back	Learn to step back and only intervene when necessary	Kishen, an NQT practitioner, worked with Abode, a shy four-year-old Nigerian boy. When Abode started to make his own puppet, the practitioner kept giving him instructions or asking him questions to 'help' him. Abode soon lost confidence or felt unable to develop his own way of making the puppet and did not want to participate.
Learners with EAL will observe play activities before they feel confident enough to join in	Try to have as many exciting artefacts and resources on display in the setting as possible (such as interactive table-top displays)	Ria tracked two EAL learners who often waited before joining in with an activity. She knew that with a little patience, she would be able to observe and record how these learners interacted at their own pace and in their own time.
Some parents of learners with EAL may not understand the purpose of playful learning	Encourage parents to work with their learners on activities in the setting on arrival to gain an idea of the different ways in which learning can take place	Grace put target cards on tables with various parent–learner activities so that parents could see the purpose of the given activity and how it linked in with the EYFS.
Not always having enough in-depth time to intervene and observe learners with EAL	Ensure within the planning that different tasks are undertaken by different practitioners and then find time for discussion	Pippa and Josie are Early Years practitioners who had planned specific activities to carry out with four learners with EAL. This involved observing and recording the learning over the first 10 minutes of each session in one week. Then they shared their notes to plan forward for progression. They also encouraged the learners to share what they have been learning about to gain ideas of anything they may have missed.

sensitively intervene to move the learning on. So time is always going to be at a premium in a busy setting, especially to talk with parents to share their understanding of play and how it aids learning. This is not easy given some of the practical difficulties of engagement.

Additional suggestions for overcoming challenges in play

Each learning environment is unique, and sometimes restricted by factors such as location, space, how many resources are available and how practitioners are deployed in a setting. Despite these kinds of restrictions, most Early Years settings are very creative, with clearly defined areas such as a wet area (for sand and water learning), an outdoor area, a quiet area (usually a book area) and creative role play areas (home corner/construction area). From our own research, we identified some strategies of good practice to encourage learners with EAL to integrate more in the process of play with their peers.

- For construction toys it is useful to have pictures of things that the learners can try to make.
- All play resources can be labelled (both pictures and words) for learners to become accustomed to writing.
- Have some multicultural dolls and puppets for self-initiated play.
- Have a variety of clothes from different cultures in a dressing up area, so that learners can experiment with different clothes and be accustomed to the differences from an early age.
- Practitioners need to intervene appropriately in play, and give learners with EAL practical things to do in context.
- Allow EAL learners to observe the play of their peers.
- When a new role play area has been set up, it is useful to show the group video clips of real-life experiences, so that learners can model their play which can then be followed up by a visit to the given place, or a visitor coming in to talk to the group.
- Role play areas should have as many resources as possible to allow learners with EAL to make informed choices.
- Use iPads, cameras and camcorders to record learners in play and then use the photos and videos as shared group discussions to talk about the learning that occurred.
- Go into role and model play with actions and words.

Reflecting on some of the suggestions above, it may be noticed that there is a hint of letting go, letting the learner with EAL take charge of their own learning through providing the relevant stimuli. Good practice is based on developing active, inquisitive and independent learners. As this limited list suggests, we need to create environments that promote such a development of physical and cognitive skills that can be captured on some kind of recording.

Moving from concrete to abstract modes of thinking allows these learners to start to modify their behaviour accordingly. Understanding such complex cognitive and social processes requires far deeper and systematic observations, analysed against, for example, Brostrom's (1999) play frame and psychological frame model. We need a number of different perspectives through research, as settings can be multicultural or monocultural and practitioners can be diverse, so we need to be cautious in interpreting evidence. Therefore we need more than one interpretive lens based on the context, plural or monocultural setting, and where there may be diverse or monocultural practitioners which is explored next.

Developing play in monocultural/monolingual settings

We now turn to a discussion of strategies for Early Years practitioners working in mono-lingual settings where there are very few young learners with EAL. It is the practitioner's responsibility to ensure that all learners have the maximum opportunity to use their own language if they wish to do so without feeling awkward. Drury and Robertson (2008) advise us that practitioners need to be careful not to promote the English language only because they do not share the EAL learner's home language. It is daunting when prac-titioners meet a number of different languages in their setting where there appear to be few setting-based support systems for accommodating this.

One of the most effective setting support system, according to Drury and Robertson (2008), is collaboration with different stakeholders, with the practitioners being solely in charge of their own teaching roles and responsibilities. This is to ensure that as prac-titioners, we do not perpetuate a common misconception that a learner who has EAL learns language quickly and therefore does not need much practitioner intervention. These learners' pronunciation may be more like that of a native speaker (Drury and Robertson, 2008), but their language skill development needs still remain to be devel-oped. This can be undertaken by practitioners observing learners with EAL communi-cating in different contexts and creating opportunities where talk is encouraged through open-ended and focused questions.

According to Pianta and Stuhlman (2004), this verbal exchange helps in bonding the practitioner–learner relationship. But as practitioners, it is important to understand the learners' backgrounds, and the way in which power relations between setting and home can affect such interactions (Cummins, 2000; Robinson and Diaz, 2006). Fumoto et al.'s (2007) study of practitioners' perceptions of their relationships with learners with EAL in the Early Years settings adds weight to the importance of verbal communication and practitioners' sensitivity shown towards EAL learners. Crucially, we believe that, if there is not enough communication with EAL parents, then we cannot have a better under-standing about their cultural, religious, national and linguistic backgrounds (as not all families are the same) (Worcestershire County Council, 2012), and this requires further investigation and is commented upon in other chapters in this book.

Summary

In summary, different views on play have been scrutinised through a review of recent literature and research evidence for reflection. What we have found is that there is no one definition of play as this depends very much on who is being asked – the parent, the learner or the practitioner. We have shown that there may be some tension about how to interpret the theory of play in learning, and even more challenging is how to develop consistent pedagogical approaches amongst the practitioners in meeting the specific needs of learners with EAL. It could be that practitioners lack confidence in grasping the relationship between theory and practice suggested by Santer et al. (2007). Some of the implications for developing play with learners with EAL have been considered. In this chapter, we advocate the EYFS (DfE, 2014) play-based approach to learning through a socio–cultural constructivist paradigm, but suggest that practitioners in the Early Years need to develop their own mental schema of a valued model of play informed by their experience in practice.

Reflective questions

- What might be a working definition of play, and how might it be different for learners with EAL?
- Capture and make notes through conversation on what parents of EAL learners think about the term play.
- Reflect on an experience of observing practitioner intervention with EAL learners in play. How has this observation helped in understanding the home culture through play?

References

Bateson, G. (1983) *Steps to ecology of the mind*. London: Paladin.

Brostrom, S. (1999) Drama games with 6-year-old children: possibilities and limitations, in Y. Engestrom, R. Miettinen and R. L. Punamaki (eds), *Perspectives on activity theory*, Cambridge: Cambridge University Press, pp. 250–63.

Bruce, T. (1997) *Early childhood education*. London: Hodder and Stoughton.

Bruner, J. S. (1983) *Child's talk: learning to use language*. Oxford: Oxford University Press.

Cummins, J. (2000) *Language, power and pedagogy: bilingual children in the crossfire*. Clevedon, Buffalo, Toronto, Sydney: Multilingual Matters.

Department for Children, Schools and Families (DCSF) (2009) *Building futures: believing in children: a focus on provision for black children in the early Years Foundation Stage*. DCSF. Available online on www.standards.dcsf.gov.uk (accessed July 2013).

Department for Education (DfE) (2010) *The importance of teaching: the Schools White Paper*, www.education.gov.uk/publications/standard/publicationDetail/Page1/CM%207980 (accessed November 2012).

Department for Education (DfE) (2014) *Statutory framework for the Early Years Foundation Stage (EYFS)*. London: DfE.

Drury, R. and Robertson, L. (2008) *Strategies for Early Years practitioners*. Reading: NALDIC.

Ethnic Minority Traveller and Refugee Achievement Service (EMTRAS) (2011) *Supporting learners for whom English is an additional language*. ('The Blue Book'). Newcastle: Newcastle City Council.

Fumoto, H., Hargreaves, D. J. and Maxwell, S. (2007) Teachers' perceptions of their relationships with children who speak English as an additional language in early childhood settings. *Journal of Early Childhood Research*, 5(2): 135–53.

Johnston, J. and Nomad-Williams, L. (2009) *Early childhood studies*. London: Pearson.

Khurana, S. (2014) School quotes: remember the good old school days with school quotes, http://quotations.about.com/od/moretypes/a/School-Quotes.htm (accessed May 2014).

Meckley, A. (2002) Observing children's play: mindful methods. Paper presented to the International Toy Research Association, London, 12 August 2002.

Montessori, M. (1912) *The Montessori method*. London: Heinemann.

National Association for Language Development in the Curriculum (NALDIC) (2012) *EYFS and EAL: supporting bilingual children in the Early Years*, www.naldic.org.uk/eal-teaching-and-learning/outline-guidance/early-years (accessed November 2013).

Office for Standards in Education (Ofsted) (2012) *English as an Additional Language: briefing for section 5 inspection*, ref. 090164, www.ofsted.gov.uk/resources/110096 (accessed April 2014).

Piaget, J. (1962) *Play, dreams and imitation in childhood*. New York: Norton.

Pianta, R. C. and Stuhlman, M. (2004) Teacher–child relationships and children's success in the first years of school. *School Psychology Review*, 33(3): 444–58.

Reed, M. and Canning, N. (eds) (2010) *Reflective practice in the Early Years*. London: Sage.

Robinson, K. H. and Diaz, J. (2006) *Diversity and difference in early childhood education: issues for theory and practice*. Maidenhead: Oxford University Press.

Santer, J., Griffiths, C. and Goodall, D. (2007) *Free play in early childhood: a literature review*. London: Play England and the National Children's Bureau.

Skinner, B. F. (1953) *Science and Human Behaviour*. London: Macmillan.

Smilansky, S. (1990) Sociodramatic play: its relevance to behaviour and achievement in schools, in E. Klugman and S. Smilansky (eds), *Children's play and learning: perspectives and policy implications*. New York: Teachers' College Press.

Vygotsky, L. (1962) *Thought and language*. Cambridge, MA: MIT Press.

Wood. E. and Attfield, J. (2006) *Play, learning and the early childhood curriculum*. 2nd edn. London: PCP.

Worcestershire County Council (2012) EAL toolkit: feeling safe, settled and valued, www.edulink.networcs.net (accessed October 2013).

Chapter 7

Using resources for learners with EAL

'The principal goal of education is to create individuals who are capable of doing new things, not simply of repeating what other generations have done – individuals who are creative, inventive and discoverers.'

Adapted from Jean Piaget (Home education, 2014)

The aims of this chapter

- To look at what kinds of resources are used effectively for Early Years pedagogy
- To critically review how such resources are planned and organised to support learner experiences
- To show how a variety of resources can be used to engage and motivate learners with EAL

Overview

The use of resources in Early Years is essential to support the learning and development of all learners through first-hand experiences in relation to the EYFS (2014) curriculum. Resources used for play are generally inclusive and gender neutral, but critical to support learning opportunities that promote skills such as collaboration and communication which are imperative for later life. Sometimes learners with EAL may not have had the opportunity to interact with certain setting resources such as play dough and stickle bricks, especially if they are new EAL arrivals. This chapter looks at what types of resources are useful and how they can be used effectively pedagogically for learners with EAL. It then goes on to discuss how they are organised for effective learning through creative approaches by practitioners. The discussion then focuses on good practice in using such resources to engage and motivate learners with EAL. This is based on the four principles underpinning the EYFS alongside four key themes of resource management. Finally, we consider some of the challenges and opportunities associated with the use of resources.

Key words: resources, communication, collaboration, pedagogy

Introduction

Quality Early Years resources can transform learning and the learning environment into an exciting and vibrant experience which stimulates learners and develops greater enthusiasm. A well-resourced Early Years setting will develop the foundation of knowledge, skills and ideas for future learning by offering as many practical first-hand experiences as possible. According to Reading Borough Council Equality Services (2010), there are few systematic quality resources to aid the learning of learners with EAL specifically. What little is available is very much focused on developing the language competency of new EAL arrivals. This is of course relevant, but does not form the total educational experience of the EAL learner. So this may cause some tension as to how best to cater for the individual needs of new EAL arrivals and especially those with specific needs identification.

Where practitioners offer a secure, safe and stimulating learning with a range of resources, this may maximise learning for all learners. There is no special adjustment required to meet the needs of learners with EAL; however, it might be useful, where possible and in some circumstances, to have interpreters at hand to aid communication. An effective learning environment can offer learners with EAL those resources that they are familiar with to support the learning process in a given context. For example, this may be materials such as colourful saris in the home corner or activities that involve playing with familiar utensils or interacting with other learners through play. Good learning happens when the learners make their own choices about which resources to use, how to use them and when to use them. As noted in other chapters, learners will try things out on their own, and time and space should be allowed for learners to experiment and take risks. As practitioners, we need to ensure support for their ideas through offering a variety of resources, and giving plenty of time and opportunities for learners with EAL to mix and play with different learners in the setting. Therefore we begin by considering the types of resources that can be used for learners with EAL.

Choosing resources to use with learners with EAL

A learning environment should mirror some aspects of the home environment to give learners a sense of security and familiarity. To that end, some of the resources listed below may assist in that home–setting link. In the Hindu culture, for example, there are special occasions on which to celebrate religious and cultural events such as Holi (a spring festival and therefore traditionally time to use lot of colour) or to make shapes called rangoli (Indian) patterns (linked to the festival of Diwali) to signify the home coming of the gods Rama and Sita from banishment into a forest for many years. This offers helpful opportunities to do activities related to making shapes and patterns inside and outside the setting which can also be linked to Mathematics (DfE, 2014). In addition, rangoli patterns can be made from powder paint, flour, rice, pasta or lentils. By making different shapes, learners will gain knowledge about shapes, classifying, sorting and describing different shapes. Some learners with EAL may also want to talk in their home language to describe shapes or numbers. They will also learn about some of the cultural traditions from storytelling, play acting or having older learners act out the Diwali story.

Such activities form a natural part of the EYFS curriculum without it being seen as a tokenistic gesture of other cultural celebrations. Through play and exploration, learners will grasp an understanding of the resource itself as some EAL learners may have already seen, made and used these resources at home. We can extend EAL learners' understanding of vocabulary using vocabulary games (items in the kitchen/bathroom/prayer area) or cutting shapes of furniture from magazines or matching shapes to words which help to decode their knowledge and understanding more deeply, as shown in Case study 7.1.

Case study 7.1

Julianne, Keetan and Suchet are four-year-olds from Finland with some basic English language understanding. A practitioner sat with them to do an activity that would develop their confidence in collaborative conversations. This involved describing, sorting and classifying pictures of people from all backgrounds. There was a lot of talk, initially in Finnish with few words of English. The practitioner sensitively probed the group through open-ended questions (such as 'Is this a girl or boy?' 'Who is this?' 'What are they wearing?') to extend their thinking and powers of describing things using a few words of English. The learners enjoyed this as it was made to be a fun activity with little intervention by the practitioner to stop the natural flow of talk. This activity was later extended to sort and classify photos of family faces and guess-the-person games to further extend learners' talking ability.

Case study 7.1 suggests that the more opportunities the learners with EAL are given for talk using a range of resources and activities (which can be as basic as pictures and photographs initially), the more they acquire new vocabulary, become more skilled and more knowledgeable, and are able to participate more competently and more independently in settings.

In developing an understanding of how resources enable learning to happen, we look at Fisher's guidance (cited in Wood and Attwood, 2006: 133) to see how resources can be utilised to develop the cognitive skills of learners which we have adapted for learners with EAL in Table 7.1. Fisher suggests that learners can be involved in the planning and arranging process to support their own learning journey.

The examples in Table 7.1 demonstrate that there are all kinds of everyday resources that help to engage learners from all EAL backgrounds and abilities, especially in the Early Years. In addition, the use of dual texts, multicultural displays, signs and symbols that are used in all kinds of settings, whether there are large minority groups of learners or not, are also seen as valuable resources. However, practitioners are well aware that at times learners who have EAL may need time just to observe other learners using resources before they have enough understanding and confidence to be able to join in. One way to speed up this process may be for practitioners to model the use of as many visual resources as possible in different contexts linked to different areas of learning through adult-initiated play. This shows good practice as it enables learners with EAL to experiment using a range of resources correctly and safely. This may help learners with EAL to make connections to the English language, and support the transference of skills to other areas of learning. In brief, learners with EAL need time and space to explore their resources and we argue that culturally diverse resources may help to develop their interest and motivation. Opportunities for 'hands-on' and 'brain-on' (Wood and Attwood, 2006: 156) activities should be provided through sensitively engaging practitioners who help make effective learning happen. Next we look at how resources can be used to support aspects of the EYFS curriculum.

Table 7.1 Managing resources for learners with EAL

Resource area	For learners with EAL
Using outdoor space like a setting playground	Key areas of learning need to be clear in the setting with appropriate resources in each area. Some resources should also be multicultural in nature such as dolls/puppets, clothes in the dressing up area, etc.
Labelling work on display board (like a visual timetable)	Labels in different home languages if necessary, and some resources should be easily accessible by all learners to promote independent choice
Using a variety of resources from home or the setting	Resources including those brought from home like tava (a round metal plate used for cooking chapattis), a spice container (with turmeric and other spices covered with cellophane or a lid so as to form a protective seal), a pretend wood-fired oven for pizzas
Sorting and classifying the categorisation of resource materials	These can be resources linked to a kitchen (where different items can be used to cook different foods), or food (where different items are eaten in different homes), or clothes (where different clothes are worn by different communities)
Creating imaginary resource areas	An opportunity to create a supermarket area with foods from around the world, or a clothes area with clothes and accessories from different cultures
Displaying resources in the setting	Use of table-top display that all learners can contribute to, which can also be a used as a show and tell area with parents when learners come into the setting first thing in the morning

Use of resources to support the EYFS

The EYFS (DfE, 2012) is underpinned by four key principles: each learner is unique; working with parents; an enabling environment; and learners develop differently and at different rates. One key feature of these principles is the importance of active learning through the effective use of resources to help raise attainment. Next, we unpick these principles against examples of how resources can be used for learners with EAL to help support practice.

Each learner is unique (resource: a wooden train)

This principle means that as practitioners our role is to develop self-assured, confident and independent individuals. We can do this for learners with EAL by giving praise with a smile or a thumbs-up gesture for achievements no matter how small or even with smiley face stickers (which are universal). For example, an experienced practitioner observed Jai, a three-year-old Iranian boy, over a fifteen-minute period. She noticed Jai looking at a group of four learners in the classroom playing with a wooden toy train resource. A wheel had come off this toy train and they were trying to fix it. Everyone had their own ideas. None could fix the wheel as they were not co-operating with each other. Jai took courage and joined in, saying that he knew how to fix the wheel. It meant using a small piece of paper wrapped around the axle to help re-attach it to the toy. It worked. Everyone was then able to play, with Jai seen as the hero. The other learners praised him for his effort and problem-solving skills. The practitioner praised him with a smiley face sticker, noticing how Jai had displayed his individuality and self-assuredness to help others in this activity. This example shows that the practitioner had given learners responsibility in the setting to experiment and explore, and the space and time for Jai to intervene, at his own pace, in encouraging collaboration, hence highlighting that each learner is unique.

Working with parents (resource: a visit to the zoo)

Zahara, a five-year-old, went to the zoo with her grandma and her little sister Maryam. Both girls were very excited at what they saw. They took photographs of the animals, saw what they ate and observed how they played with other animals. Zahara took the photographs into her setting and the practitioner helped her to share her day's experiences at the zoo with other learners. Zahara was delighted to share her experiences with much work and learning coming from the visit. So through co-operation with the parents/family, the visit to the zoo acted as a good learning resource.

Such situations may be common practice in Early Years settings and help to continue to foster good home–setting relations. During the visit, both grandma and Zahara were able to talk in Punjabi and English, with the visit to the zoo acting as catalyst for developing language. Research has shown that learners as young as two years old are able to speak different languages and are able to switch between languages appropriately with individuals (Devarakonda, 2013). The authors of this book can confirm this, both being multilingual, and switching from Punjabi to English or Gujerati to English when they were very young. What is equally important is to ensure that Zahara is encouraged to learn English without losing her first language and with the support and encouragement of her parents.

An enabling environment (a range of resources)

One example of ways in which an enabling environment can be created is through offering a variety of clothing items in the dressing-up area. For example, a practitioner in a reception setting was observing four-year-old Vina in the dressing-up area which had been converted to a clothes shop. Vina is originally from Mombasa, and although she had some understanding of the English language, her first language was Swahili. The practitioner observed Vina interacting with other learners in the dressing-up area as they were pretending to be fairies floating around (which stemmed from a story stimulus earlier in the day). As they moved their arms around, Vina did not seem too happy with her dressing-up clothes. So she went into the fabric box and whilst talking to herself in Swahili she took out a large square scarf and made it into a cape around her, which made it easier to pretend to fly. Her peers also copied her, and began to pretend to fly to different places. Other examples include being encouraged to use the same resources indoors and outdoors to encourage language development (such as construction blocks, scissors, felt pens, paints, books to share, sand and water trays), and setting up a varied range of interactive table-top displays to promote collaborative conversations. This setting encouraged learners to access a range of resources in addition to those placed in areas to support and extend their learning. For learners with EAL it means they should be encouraged to share their own resources from home which may be culturally different to those of indigenous learners. Investing in different resources may help learners to celebrate differences, and through this enabling environment and using high quality Early Years resources, learners with EAL may become more competent learners.

Learners develop differently and at different rates (modelling use of resources)

Through observations practitioners will gain an idea as to what learners' prior experience is with the usage of resources. Therefore when selecting resources, the understanding that learners develop and learn in different ways and at different times (DfE, 2012: 3) means that as practitioners we have to be mindful of the appropriateness of the resources we use. One way to ensure this is through modelling their use for learners with EAL. For example, Vijay was a learner with EAL and a new arrival from Sri Lanka. He arrived in the nursery setting in April, and understood some words in English such as car, train, bat and ball. On arrival at the setting he would always choose to go outdoors and play with the cars, bikes, and other outdoor equipment such as the fixed slide. However, when it came to learning that involved technology, Vijay would retreat into the silent phase and not respond, especially when other learners used the interactive whiteboard or iPads. Through observations, the practitioners realised that unless they modelled the use of technology, Vijay seemed to be reluctant to use it in supporting learning, which in turn would have an impact on his technological development. During discussions with his parents it came to light that they could not afford the modern technological items that seemed to be the norm in many learners' homes, such as iPhones and iPads. This means that as practitioners we need to remind ourselves that not all learners will have access to the same kinds of resources in their home environment, which in turn will have an impact on their starting point in development at the setting. Naturally those learners with greater opportunities in the home environment will be more confident using certain resources.

Another way that resources can be modelled is through allowing learners to model them to each other or showing video clips of how resources can be used. For learners with EAL this means taking stock of stages of growth and development mapped against appropriate use of resources, for example, to assessing what resources are suitable to develop the language of learners with EAL at the pre-conceptual stage of around two to four years, or at the third stage, the intuitive stage of two to seven years, when operations such as classifying, ordering and quantifying are developed, but they may not be able to explain why yet. Here, re-visiting some of the development psychologists' views may be helpful, such as those of Piaget, Vygotsky and Bruner.

We now turn to four themes of managing resources in Early Years to further develop learning opportunities especially for learners with EAL, namely Human, Physical, Indoor verses Outdoor and Managing Creatively with a smaller space. Each of these has its own advantages and disadvantages which will be discussed, as well as suggestions to improve practice.

Human resources

High quality staff are the most valuable resource any setting has, especially in Early Years where there is a higher practitioner–learner ratio. All learners achieve more when they feel happy, safe and secure. Early Years practitioners are in a unique position to develop each learner's self-esteem by building upon what their learners can do through play and other contextual creative ways, which may not be possible outside this age phase owing to pressures associated with testing and results. This approach is reliant on sound educational theory like those of Piaget (2005), Bruner (1986), Vygotsky on social learning theories (1978), Gagne and Deci on self-determination and motivation (2005), Bandura (1977), Rogers on humanistic approach to psychology (see Thorne and Sanders, 2013) and Bruce (2012). To become confident independent learners, learners need consistency. This is often provided through the daily routine, the organisation of the learning environment and resources, and good practitioner–learner interaction. Effective use of human resources to support good learning is facilitated by knowing the learners with EAL well and knowing the best resources to be used to aid their learning.

For example, plan activities for learners with EAL based on what they know already (which may be a lower starting point in comparison with the rest of the group) and how learning will aid their attainment and progress. Rogers et al. (2013) talk about experiential learning where the role of the practitioner is to facilitate such learning for all learners, which depends on how much time practitioners have with them, what learning environment are accessible (indoor versus outdoor) and how many learners there are. Bandura (1977) considers that we need to ensure a balance of approach in teaching and learning that is based on interaction between cognitive, behavioural and environmental influences. This means the resources should be fit for purpose to maximise such interactions for the learners with EAL. It also means that where the resources are meaningful to the learners' experiences, they will more likely see meaning when involved in discovery which is essential for learners with EAL.

Some of the advantages of good quality human resources specifically in Early Years include having practitioners who are knowledgeable about the context and philosophy of Early Years, good knowledge and understanding about the EYFS and therefore making connections in learning look seamless for learners with EAL, and also having the skills to construct activities in a variety of ways to support the silent phase of new EAL arrivals. Having a stable Early Years team who know their learners and the context very well is important so that planning is more personalised to individual needs. However, one of the key disadvantages of human resources in the context of this chapter is practitioners who lack knowledge of working with learners who have EAL. If this is the case, it is useful to seek support from another nearby setting with a higher proportion of learners with EAL to share ideas of good practice and support. This is also one way to begin new partnerships between settings, regardless of whether they are rural or urban. In addition, we offer the following suggestions to further promote human resources to facilitate learning for learners with EAL.

1   Encourage practitioners to observe learners with EAL at different stages of language comprehension to see if the same judgements apply in all contexts (formal, play, indoor, outdoor).
2   Discuss with the setting leader how planning has been personalised to meet the needs of learners with EAL, what their role would be to support this process, and how they could be challenged further.
3   Encourage all practitioners to be visible to the parents as much as possible to aid recognition of roles and also to build relationships so that not all questions/concerns

are directed to the setting leader all the time – this encourages a shared culture and more teamwork in the setting.

We already know that good quality practitioners are key to the success of any setting. However, we also need to consider the importance of parents as a human resource as their support is crucial, especially in the early stages of education. Therefore we move on to considering how parents can be utilised for learners with EAL to support the human resource theme.

Parents as a resource

Parents can be a great asset for bringing in material resources or, as parents of learners with EAL, to be asked to join in with specific events and celebrations to add to a rich learning environment. It is important to ensure that all learners and parents feel welcomed, respected and valued. Many parents of learners with EAL may be able to share their experiences to raise awareness of similarities and differences in 'culture, religion, background, circumstances and issues that may have led to the exclusion of children due to prejudice or discrimination in the past' (Devarakonda, 2013: 42). Having a better understanding of these families arguably leads to a more inclusive environment for all.

In one setting, it was observed that all parents in Early Years and Key Stage One were encouraged to come into the setting a little earlier than the official setting start time so that they could settle their learner, but also so that the learner could share what they can do with the resources set out on the tables. This was especially valuable for those learners with EAL as parents would ask questions in their home language, and the learners would rapidly explain everything that they are expected to do. In addition, it was useful for the setting practitioners to observe that for learners with EAL the silent phase is demonstrated during the day, yet, in conversations observed with the parent at home time, their understanding of routine and use of resources was evident. In addition to direct translation parents can therefore support the use of resources in a setting in many ways – especially for those learners who have EAL. The following are some examples.

1   Use of different dressing-up clothes/kitchen dishes in the home corner – and parents encouraged to join in with play first thing in the morning to help link resources to context, e.g. helping their learners to wear clothes like they may do, such as tying a headscarf, or wearing a turban, or wrapping a sari/kimono.
2   Encourage the use of key words in other languages (such as hello and goodbye), and use them with the parents, e.g. especially during meet and greet in the morning with families and their learners.
3   Have a parents' board with labels and signs in the home language to aid communication such as welcome signs, and basic setting information, e.g. book change day, special setting events. The format of a visual timetable may also support this suggestion.
4   Allow learners to bring in music from home to share with others in the setting, therefore broadening cultural knowledge; this can either be a learner-initiated activity in the listening area or it can be more formal through the Expressive Arts and Design area of learning in the EYFS.

5   Try different cultural foods during snack times in line with dietary requirements. For example, Simran, who is Priti's mum, was laying out some snacks for a party at a setting which included some samosas (traditional Indian savoury). This then led to play in the home corner through the observed dialogue below:

Priti: Mummy, let's play cooking.
Simran: OK, let me finish the snack food then I will come over.

(Priti goes to the home corner which is set up as a kitchen and asks some peers there if they want to play cooking with her.)

Priti: Let's all play cooking. What shall we make?
Simran (goes over): What shall we make, Priti?
Priti: I want to make samosas. Let's have some peas ones – I like them.
Simran: These samosas have peas and potatoes in them anyway.
Priti: OK. Let's have some lamb ones too.

Such an interaction involved Priti, a four-year-old Gujerati girl in planning for her snack through pretend cooking. She knew about the food she wanted with support from her mum. This learning journey can be developed further by encouraging parents and their learners to take photographs at home of different foods they eat which can be used for collaborative conversations at the setting.

6   Try to expose all learners to as many diverse practitioners and parents as possible so that learners are used to different kinds of people. For example, a practitioner had told her group a story about her holiday abroad with supporting photographs and souvenirs. She then invited three parents in who had been on holidays to Nairobi in Kenya, Jullundur in Punjab and Kerala in south India during the summer holidays. After the parents had told their story, each of their learners could then tell their peers more about their individual interests in what they saw, what they ate and what they liked the most. This provoked much interest, collaborative talk and creative work. The practitioner made good use of pictures cut out from holiday brochures to talk about numbers, about creative development through using puppets as one of the EAL learner had seen a street show in Jullundur, and other activities using a range of resources to do art, music, dance, role play and imaginative play.

7   Table-top displays of specific resources associated with festivals and celebrations so that all learners become used to the purpose of different resources and their impacts on culture. For example, four-year-old Manju had brought in some artefacts from home after her dad had been to Turkey on a business trip. Manju brought in a collection of badges, bracelets, coloured stones, a small brooch and lots of photographs of colourful and beautifully shaped buildings. The practitioner helped her to put these as a display on a table with books about Turkey, a magnifying glass, labels and trays. The learners enjoyed guessing what some of the artefacts were with the help of problem-solving and open-ended questions. Such creative displays offer opportunities to use resources imaginatively and aid learners' communication skills. According to DfES (2007), these strategies help learners to continue to be interested, excited and motivated to learn. They also assist them in using language imaginatively to express their thoughts and feelings.

This is not a definitive list of using resources, as there are many more strategies that will come with time and experience. The key point is how this information is used to inform planning to help meet the needs of learners with EAL as well as broadening the knowledge and experience of other learners too. Next we focus on physical resources in the setting.

Physical resources

Every Early Years setting has a range of age- and development-appropriate physical resources for most areas of learning. The unique aspect of Early Years is that the physical resources also incorporate outdoor equipment such as climbing frames, large building blocks and sunken pits. There are a whole range of physical resources that are useful for learners with EAL ranging from multicultural puppets and characters linked to topics and areas of learning, to the use of ICT which can be used both indoors and outdoors. However, what is important to note is how interactive tools such as the interactive whiteboards, visualisers, and iPads help to 'weave the practitioner and learner' to help raise learners' understanding (Laudrum and Chynoweth, 2012: 100). In other words, practitioners need to continue to consider how learners are helped to make connections between areas of learning and their own experiences. For learners with EAL this means providing a creative and exciting learning environment through use of varied resources that they can touch (bumpy/smooth, soft/rough) and smell (sweet/spicy) to develop communication ability. One example of this is through the use of table-top displays that learners are encouraged to add to, which promote collaborative conversations through the freedom to handle the resources on the table.

Table 7.2 offers examples of ways in which physical resources can be used in creative ways for learners with EAL, with suggested links to areas of the EYFS.

Again, it is important to first observe how learners with EAL use the resources provided which gives practitioners an idea of their starting point, before intervention through modelling takes place. It is also important to be mindful of some of the considerations for physical resources presented below.

- Do learners with EAL know how to use the equipment or does it need to be modelled, especially items such as scissors and threading beads?
- Are learners clear about their expectations in the safe use of the given equipment such as large outdoor apparatus?
- How can using certain resources be linked to several areas of learning such as ICT?

However, we also need to be aware of some of the possible disadvantages of physical resources, including asking: Do all have access to them, especially when budgets are so tight? With a huge variety of resources available, what is cost effective and meets more than one area of learning through enhancing the resources already available? Table 7.3 shows one example of how some physical resources have been used specifically with EAL learners in a reception setting in the outdoor environment when budgets for resources are limited.

Our aim is that Table 7.3 offers a template of one plan to start an activity, but as practitioners reflect on theories of learning, they will note that by allowing learners to investigate for themselves, they will take their own lead in seeing what the mini-beast does, thus doing their own research.

Table 7.2 Use of resources to develop learning of learners with EAL

Resource area	Ideas for learners with EAL	Link to area of learning in the EYFS
Role play	Combination of puppets/characters, dressing-up clothes (with supporting pictures), specific theme-related artefacts/toys.	A well-planned role-play area through set topics provides rich opportunities for developing Communication and Language, and Literacy, and offering purposes for writing, reading, speaking and listening.
Creative	Range of materials that include scissors, glue, wrapping/shiny paper, fabric, sequences, buttons, wool, play dough, plasticine and junk modelling materials.	Making links to Understanding the World through discussions of various materials: how light is reflected through shiny materials, how force is used with manipulating materials such as play dough, and how junk modelling can link to Expressive Arts and Design through model making.
Shared reading	Combination of large and small books (which include pop-up and picture books) with associated puppets and dual texts (if applicable).	Collaborative discussions with both practitioners and other learners about characters in a book and puppets, links to Communication and Language. Providing stimulus for discussion with supporting questions is vital to engage learners to develop systematic synthetic phonics and vocabulary.
Mark making	Use of a variety of papers, whiteboards, small notebooks including tracing letters and paper. Also a variety of writing equipment: felt tips (large and small), pencils, wax crayons and pencil crayons so that learners are encouraged to mark make and write.	By using items such as large felt tips or play dough, learners are encouraged to mark make in a creative way. Another example to support the area of Literacy is to use smaller trays of sand, flour or small pulses to encourage learners to form letters, promoting the correct finger and wrist movement.
Numbers	Use of large dice, number cards, dominoes, bingo, interactive whiteboards and iPads with number games to promote calculations and correct terminology.	There are many games that could support Mathematics in different ways such as using the parachute outside and using the numbers on some dice to be added or subtracted. Or using larger hoops in the setting to match objects to numbers to help with visual representation.
Sand	Wet and dry sand, which can be coloured, or can have other items such as glitter/sparkles, rice, etc. added to it to help stimulate imagination when used with sand equipment.	This can support discussions in Understanding the World regarding how resources such as sand change when water is added. This could also be applied to other resources such as flour, salt and sugar.
Water	Adding different textures such as a little ice in the summer and snow in the winter, glitter/sparkles, dry pulses. Add colour or bath foam for sensory exploration.	This will support discussion in the Personal Social and Emotional Development area of learning in terms of how hands feel when ice/pasta/cornflour are added to water.

Large construction	Items include: mega blocks, large building blocks, megaformers, building sets, meccano, marble runs, etc., with supporting pictures for ideas that can be constructed.	This links to all areas of learning and supports a learner's gross motor skills, teamwork and having the freedom to work either alone or as part of a group.
Small construction	Items include: stickle bricks, small building blocks, train/road tracks with transport, lego, with support picture to aid imagination.	This links to all areas of learning and supports fine motor skills and discussions linked to the setting topic and the reinforcement of topic-related vocabulary.
Exploration and investigation	Linked to theme, e.g. magnifying glass for mini-beasts (stick insects, tadpoles in tanks), soil trays, toy mini-beasts with supporting pictures, key words and books on a table-top display. Other ideas include remote control toys with large map/track/town mats to aid collaborative conversations.	Discussions through using the resources suggested support all areas of learning, but in particular Understanding the World through key questions to further learners' understanding.
Small world	Small world items such as people, animals, threading beads, jigsaw puzzles, board games, cars.	The resources here support fine motor skills including finger and hand co-ordination.
Outdoor	Combination of fixed large apparatus to develop gross motor skills, and changeable toys linked to themes or seasons. Sand/water/chalk/paint easels can be brought outside. Mats and cushions are also useful for an outdoor quiet space.	A lot of the resources suggested will link to learners' prior experience and confidence especially through the usage of large outdoor fixed equipment. This supports many areas of learning through specific topic links, but more generally through Personal, Social and Emotional Development.

Learners with EAL can quickly learn the vocabulary when associated with a picture. So when planning for reading, a wide variety of ordinary and dual language books could be used. Thus when the practitioner is reading a story using visual clues in the book, learners with EAL can practice voicing certain words in order to develop speaking and listening skills as demonstrated by Case study 7.2.

Case study 7.2

Deepak is an experienced Early Years practitioner and a keen musician, being a member of the local Bhangra dance group. He was reading a story about musical instruments from other countries and was showing and telling a small group of learners with EAL about the dholl (a large cylindrical drum often worn suspended from around the neck, with the side skins of the dholl beaten with a short curved stick).

(continued)

(continued)

Listening skills was the focus of the session. After listening to the story and watching how the dholl was played, these learners were able to share many experiences as some of them had been to Hindu or Sikh weddings where such dholl playing and Bhangra dancing was the norm. So as it was within their lived experiences they easily grasped words like dholl and Bhangra. Following on from the story, the learners made drawings of the dholl, made a similar-sized model through junk modelling to produce a variety of sounds, and explained how the model was made and what materials were used (using descriptive language); they discussed plans and worked collaboratively. Two learners from the group extended their learning by choosing to do a Bhangra dance (Physical Development, EYFS; DfE, 2014), very successfully.

Case study 7.2 shows that where a setting extends the personal, social and cultural experiences of the learners with EAL as shown here, the likelihood of engagement with learning becomes heightened.

The discussion now moves on the importance of indoor versus outdoor play. In an ideal world, both learning environments should have equal importance, but historically learning in the indoor environment has always been given greater importance and status.

Table 7.3 A case study example of using resources to develop communication skills

Aim	To look at investigating mini-beasts in the local setting grounds
Learning objectives	To identify a range of mini-beasts verbally in both English and the learners' home languages To begin to develop vocabulary of scientific words like describing body shape, has legs/no legs, has wings/no wings
Context	In the outdoor environment table-top displays were set up. One table had black sugar paper and some snails on it, another table had soil trays with magnifying glasses, another table had plastic tanks with tadpoles. To support the learning objectives, the practitioner left this as a learner-initiated activity with selected input from the practitioner after a prior discussion and some modelling about treating mini-beasts safely and with respect. The role of the practitioner was to observe the link to language identification of EAL learners through interaction with other EAL peers on each table, including a free-choice digging area.
Learning observed	In this first-hand activity, learners became absorbed and even excited at observing the mini-beasts. The practitioner found that in some cases there were no direct translations for words such as beetles, etc.; instead a generic term was used by some EAL learners from a Gujerati background (such as dudu, which is a generic Swahili term for insects) for all mini-beasts. In this case new terminology had to be introduced with supporting photographs that were taken.

Resources: indoor versus outdoor play

Planning for learning in different environments, namely, the outdoor and indoor, requires the provision to be organised so that learners are offered opportunities to work individually, in pairs or groups, or with a practitioner (Drake, 2010: 7). The planning therefore has to be closely allied to consideration of resources (Woods, 2013: preface). We now turn to the literature to look at some background information in relation to the resource impact of creating an outdoor (Cartwright *et al.*, 2005; Ambrose and Armstrong, 2009) and indoor learning environment. The conceptual thrust from Cartwright *et al.* (2005: 7) is on using resources to 'develop learning environments which promote independence and autonomy' and 'attentive and engaged practitioners' models of practice. Bilton (2010: 44) has identified the different types of outdoor provision and Waite *et al.*'s (2008) argument supports the assumption that learners do not just learn what they are taught, rather, they learn through experience in which resources are essential. The importance of the use of resources in purposeful play (both indoor and outdoor) is also acknowledged by the EYFS (DfE, 2012: 6: 1.9). The indoor learning environment, like the outdoor provision, offers opportunities to provide learning spaces with equipment and materials to support practice, as shown in Table 7.4.

Table 7.4 also suggests that it is important for learners with EAL to recognise the type/tone of language and gestures used to encourage, motivate and enthuse engagement

Table 7.4 How indoor and outdoor resources can support learning

For learners with EAL	Indoor learning resources	Outdoor learning resources
Context 1: after a visit to a local zoo, Kamaljit Kaur, a higher-ability Sikh girl aged five years old, was interested in developing an indoor lions' den after seeing this at the zoo (choice and independence)	Using animal puzzles to identify other animals in the zoo Using animal puppets to go into role play	Using larger construction blocks and large fabric pieces to create her own lions' den Using zoo animal masks to go into role play outdoors
Context 2: after walking to school one frosty morning, three-year-old Raj was telling the practitioner at the setting that the ground was crunchy on the way.	Leaves collected were used to create prints with paints. Leaf shapes were also made using handprints	Learners were taken for a walk around the setting to develop their vocabulary in relation to walking through autumnal leaves, which were also collected for a setting display
Context 3: after a story stimulus (*Going on a Bear Hunt*) four-year-old Rohan was telling the practitioner that he was trying to find a bear in the setting to use for going on a bear hunt	Teddy bears were used to go on a teddy bears picnic Snack items such as plates and cups were used to support the picnic	An obstacle course can be created using larger blocks and mats to create aspects of the story outside Learners can use teddy bears to go into role outside where the environment can seem more real

with, and through purposeful play resources for enjoyment in, both indoor and outdoor environments. If a setting does not have an outdoor area, then explore an outdoor environment near a setting, like a woodland which is safe and secure and allows learners to interact with each other through playing and problem-solving. In one nursery setting, the authors of this book interviewed four Early Years practitioners working with learners from three months to five years of age about their perception of the outdoor classroom for learners who have EAL. Many commented that the outdoor environment enabled the learners to be more active. Learners were more excited and also more explorative, especially those with EAL, many of whom did not have these outdoor experiences, which supported Cartwright et al.'s (2005) finding that outdoor learning stimulated exploration and investigation. However, before we continue to highlight the importance of outdoor play in supporting intellectual stimulation and imagination (Bruce, 2012), let us also consider some of the challenges in resourcing an outdoor environment.

Some of these same Early Years practitioners in the nursery setting agreed with what Cartwright et al. (2005) suggested in terms of the challenges in providing outdoor learning, especially for those who have EAL in order to increase their English language competency. These challenges included:

- having a low provision of practitioners and therefore not enough to be both indoors and outdoors,
- a lack of age/stage-appropriate activities to be used outside,
- limited resources and experiences to explore all curriculum areas outside, and
- ineffective use of features within the environment (such as a flower/vegetable patch or pond).

One way to overcome some of these resourcing challenges facing an Early Years setting was to create an action improvement plan which was well received by all practitioners. The action improvement plan had specific planned outcomes, such as introducing a new outdoor planning framework, reassessing the role of the practitioner in the facilitation of outdoor experiences, increasing opportunities for targeted individual/group activities, enhancing the quality of teaching and learning in outdoor provision, creating more opportunities for creative, sensory and exploratory play and providing stretch and challenge activities to support development. These actions made a big difference as practitioners were working more as a team, in collegial ways, to exchange ideas to best serve the needs of their learners, especially those with EAL.

Bilton (2010) suggests that learning outside can be harder than inside, one may be physically more active, regularly battling against the elements and often more alert – watchful for potential dangers. Being involved in play and constantly mindful of play possibilities can be mentally exhausting. Overall, learning outdoors is physically and mentally more challenging. Our concerted efforts show that the learners will benefit in the end. In the findings of a survey conducted by Jane (nursery leader) involving the Early Years practitioners, the practitioners found that facilitating outdoor learning was exhausting but worth the time and effort when the learners show signs that they are happily making progress in their learning. One practitioner in this setting commented that it was wonderful to see learners with EAL interacting with others in a context they felt was fun. We now move on to seeing how resources can be managed creatively.

Managing resources creatively within a small space

Some Early Years practitioners are restricted in terms of the type of learning environment they would like to set up and resources for their learners owing to constraints of the physical space in terms of layout and location. This also means that some Early Years settings may not even have an outdoor area if they are in an urban area where space is at a premium. Therefore some strategies for managing resources include having storage at a safe higher level (cupboards/shelves) for resources that are not needed immediately, putting table-top displays on top of low storage cupboards, using rugs in the carpet area that also double up as transport tracks/maps, use of window sills for storage and hanging displays if the security system allows it. Another option is also using the playground of the setting when not in use by older learners at playtime and lunchtime. For learners with EAL this means they can feel more secure within a small space to interact with each other and enter into conversation. In this respect, greater creativity would be required in setting up an environment with limited time, space and resources as illustrated by Case study 7.3.

Case study 7.3

Jay was a recently qualified practitioner who had specialised in Early Years at university. Her first teaching job was in a reception class in a London setting. The problem was that space was at a premium at the setting, and therefore the only outdoor space was the small playground that all the learners shared. In addition all the classrooms were the same size and therefore there was no wet area, which meant it was difficult to have sand and water trays in the classroom all the time. It also meant that there was no outdoor environment, and therefore the learning was restricted to the classroom. In order to resolve this, Jay made contact with a setting nearby (which had similar issues with space) to see how they managed their resources for learning. During her visits to this setting she learned how to use the playground in such a way that certain outdoor equipment could stay outside all the time, allowing other learners to access it too. She also learned how storage could be used in a more creative way to store resources outside (such as bikes, cars, etc.). Over time she observed how practitioners took small groups of learners outside for specific outdoor activities, which was essential for all learners, but especially for those with EAL who blossomed in a very different way in terms of their language and social development. Finally, Jay learned that the best ideas and some solutions to issues can be found through building partnerships with settings in a similar context in order to share resources and, through this, reaped the benefits for all her learners, and more specifically learners with EAL.

The challenges of managing resources

Gaining access to resources and managing them to be used safely remains a constant challenge for Early Years practitioners with limited budgets to build up indoor and outdoor resources. In addition, it is important to have different basic setting resources (such as fabric, buttons, ribbon, etc.) to allow learners the freedom to make their own resources depending on their unplanned role play and collaborative conversations that help engage learning further. The creativity of practitioners in these areas is constantly of display, as shown by the ideas in Table 7.5.

Most settings find it a challenge to find storage space or buy expensive resources. This requires a team effort to resolve such issues creatively and pragmatically through effective planning. Ambrose and Armstrong (2009) argue that practitioners need to scaffold learning with the emphasis placed on 'what to teach and what to allow children to discover alone' through supporting resources (Bilton, 2010: 44). There is also the challenge of keeping up-to-date with new resources over a period of time, especially with the time constraints that exist in settings. What needs to be done about these challenges is to think and act creatively, as a team, collaborate across settings and share each other's expertise and experiences.

Summary

In summary, we acknowledge that practitioners in Early Years already prepare resources but may need extra time devoted to learners with EAL and new arrivals. Rather than list a range of examples of activities that work for learners with EAL, we have included specific links to them, like the Equality Services booklet produced by Reading Borough Equality Services (2010). There are many resources aimed at maximising learning opportunities for all learners, and we have looked at how many of them can be adapted

Table 7.5 Ideas for how to maximise the use of limited resources to aid learning

Challenge regarding resources	Possible strategies for learners with EAL	Suggested examples
• limited budget for resources	Find out if there is a multicultural service in the area that can support with resources	Seek advice from other nearby settings to see if they can share resources
• not having enough time to be creative with resources	Involve other practitioners in the setting to share responsibility for seeing how certain resources such as sand and water can be used with EAL learners to support language terminology	Encouraging practitioners to have key vocabulary (sand, soft, lumpy, dry) and key question (what does it feel like?) cards to support resources
• lack of storage facilities	Make topic/theme boxes with pouches of resources for EAL learners (which can include action cards with supporting key words); if possible, see if any resource storage is possible in the outdoor area (lockable shed) to keep bikes, cars, etc.	Just use the theme boxes when needed; otherwise store them away to save space
• lack of practitioners to support use of resources	Learners with EAL in particular need practitioners to use the resources with them so they can observe their modelling	Practitioners use resources with the learners initially before moving away

for the learners with EAL. We have shown that appropriate context-based resource planning for learners with EAL needs to be continued by practitioners for effective learner experiences. Apart from the day-to-day physical resources for teaching and learning, like interactive whiteboards, iPads, and videos, a suggestion is made to look for 'contextual and visual support, writing frames, key visuals (graphic organiser) and bilingual resources' (Reading Borough Equality Services, 2010: 22). Using bilingual and multilingual skills of other practitioners, as well as liaison with an EAL specialist if possible, can also be invaluable human resources in providing creative equal opportunities for learners with EAL.

Reflective questions

- Reflect on the kinds of resources that can be used to encourage collaborative conversations for learners with EAL and make a note of these conversations.
- What specific physical resources does a setting use to support learners with EAL, and how are these resources linked to areas of learning?
- Consider how the use of resources outdoors can be differentiated for learners who have EAL.

Useful web sources:

We have included a list of useful web links that will give ideas for using resources in different contexts for learners with EAL. Many of these ideas can be adapted to be used beyond the Early Years setting.

General teaching resources linked to topics:
www.bestprimaryteachingresources.com/

Language resources to help with word translation for French, German and Spanish:
www.tts-group.co.uk/shops/tts/Range/EAL-Resources/86da2240-cbb0-4a8f-b9fc-581107c902d0

Learning through play resources:
www.nicurriculum.org.uk/docs/foundation_stage/learning_through_play_ey.pdf

Multilingual labels for display:
www.schoolslinks.co.uk/resources_dl.htm

NALDIC – amazing website for a range of EAL resources, ideas and support:
www.naldic.org.uk/

Resources for areas of learning in Early Years:
www.eduzone.co.uk/acatalog/index.html

Resources for role play, themes and festivals:
www.earlylearninghq.org.uk/role-play-resources/

References

Ambrose, L. and Armstrong, J. (2009) *Early Years outdoor learning: a toolkit for developing Early Years outdoor provision*. Norwich: Norfolk County Council.

Bandura, A. (1977) *Social theory learning*. New York: General Learning Press.

Bilton, H. (2010) *Outdoor learning in the Early Years: Management and Innovation*, 3rd edn. Oxford: Routledge.

Bruce, T. (2012) *Early childhood practice*. London: Sage.

Bruner, J. (1986) *Actual minds, possible worlds*. Cambridge, MA: Harvard University Press.

Carr, M. (2001) *Assessment in early childhood settings: learning stories*. London: Paul Chapman.

Cartwright, P., Scott, K. and Stevens, J. (2005) *A place to learn: developing a stimulating learning environment*. London: LEARN.

Department for Education and Skills (DfES) (2007) *The Early Years Foundation Stage: statutory framework for the Early Years Foundation Stage and practice guidance for the Early Years Foundation Stage*. London: HMSO.

Department for Education (DfE) (2012) *Early Years Foundation Stage (EYFS)*. London: DfE, https://www.education.gov.uk/publications/standard/publicationDetail/Page1/DCSF-00261-2012 (accessed 5 January 2014).

Department for Education (DfE) (2014) *Statutory framework for the Early Years Foundation Stage (EYFS)*. London: DfE.

Devarakonda, C. (2013) *Diversity and inclusion in Early Years: an introduction*. London: Sage.

Drake, J. (2010) *Planning for children's play and learning*. London: Routledge.

Fisher, J. (2002) *Starting from the child?* 2nd edn. Buckingham: Open University Press.

Gagne, M. and Deci, E. L. (2005) Self-determination theory and work motivation. *Journal of Organizational Behavior*, 26(4): 331–62.

Home education (2014) Resources – quotes, www.home-education.org.uk/resources-quotes.htm (accessed May 2014).

Laudrum, L. and Chynoweth, S. (2012) Classroom kills, in A. Cockburn and G. Handscomb (eds) *Teaching children 3–13*. London: Sage, pp. 89–107.

Piaget, J. (2005) *The child's conception of the world*. New York: Rowman and Littlefield.

Reading Borough Council Equality Services (2010) *Supporting newly arrived bilingual pupils: guidance for teachers in primary schools*. Reading: Equality Services.

Rogers, C., Lyon, R., Harold, C. and Tausch, R. (2013) *On becoming an effective teacher: person-centred teaching, psychology, philosophy, and dialogues with Carl R. Rogers and Harold Lyon*. London: Routledge.

Thorne, B. and Sanders, P. (2013) *Carl Rogers*. 3rd edn. London: Sage.

Vygotsky, L. S. (1978) *Mind in society: the development of higher psychological processes*. Cambridge, MA: Harvard University Press.

Waite, S., Davis, B. and Brown, K. (2008) *Current practice and aspirations for outdoor learning for 2–11 year olds in Devon*. Plymouth: University of Plymouth.

Wood, E. and Attwood, J. (2006) *Play, learning and the early childhood curriculum*. 2nd edn. London: Paul Chapman.

Woods, A. (2013) (ed.) *Child-initiated play and learning: planning for possibilities in the Early Years*. London: Routledge.

Chapter 8

How leaders/managers promote excellent learning environments for learners with EAL

'I suppose leadership at one time meant muscles; but today it means getting along with people.'

Mahatma Gandhi (Edberg, 2013)

The aims of this chapter

- To understand what constitutes excellent leadership and management
- To explore how different leadership and management styles are practically applied for the benefit of learners with EAL
- To look at how leaders/managers promote excellent pedagogical learning environments to support learners with EAL

Overview

Practitioners who work in Early Years settings have the greatest influence on how learning is planned, organised and executed for the benefit of learners. Leading a diverse or heterogeneous workforce is a leadership challenge in itself. However, to lead and manage effective learning for learners with EAL especially in the Early Years may require additional specific cultural and linguistic knowledge and understanding. This chapter will begin by looking at why it is important to know and understand the fine difference between leadership and management and to know how different leadership and management approaches may have an impact on learning for learners with EAL. The chapter then unfolds and analyses some of the approaches in creating excellent learning environments to promote learning for EAL learners and why it is useful for leaders to understand theories of different leadership and management styles in this context.

Key words: leadership for learning, management, leadership styles, values

Introduction

Leadership is really about power, influence and persuasion. We will reflect upon a few examples later that demonstrate how leaders use such competences to manage curriculum change and how they effectively lead the teaching and learning for learners with EAL. We are committed to the values of leadership and management that drive forward practice in Early Years. So we have added this chapter as we believe that developing the leadership abilities of practitioners is a moral imperative if they are to support learners with EAL effectively. We believe our values shown in this chapter, and indeed in the whole book, are based on social justice, democracy, the promotion of equal opportunities, inclusivity, and the valuing of diversity. With increasingly more diverse learner population in our settings regarding the cultural, ethnic and religious backgrounds of the learners, we believe it is crucial to understand how to lead and manage for diversity (Lumby *et al.*, 2005). Most of the research on developing the notions of leadership and management appears to be generally Anglocentric in its approach. This means that educational leadership and management tend to presume a 'homogeneous staff and student body'. However, Coleman and Glover (2010: 4) suggest that this is now no longer the case given England's growing multicultural population.

In the context of Early Years settings one aspect of the leadership role is to ensure that planning is effectively put in place for learners with EAL linked to the Early Learning Goals (ELGs) of the EYFS (DfE, 2014). According to Conteh (2012: 54), practitioners have to ensure that learners who are at the early stages of developing English 'learn the curriculum content' and 'use English in increasingly academic ways in order to access the curriculum'. So it is valuable for practitioners and leaders to look at resources and strategies that will maximise learning for learners with EAL grounded in meaningful and personal experiences. It is therefore important to have some firm beliefs and values about what Early Years education is about, especially for those learners who have EAL, which can be evident through the setting's ethos. More importantly, it is necessary to challenge the perception that Early Years is nothing more than play, and therefore that learning is limited.

What is equally important is to look at how Early Years leaders reflect their values in the setting to promote world-class learning through creating excellent learning environments, which is a key focus of Early Years. Values can be promoted in different ways by practitioners, parents, learners and the wider community. It is about the way practitioners talk with each other or the way they articulate their attitudes to social justice and equity and human rights principles. What we have found through our research is that teaching learners about beliefs and values through the EYFS has to be modelled and debated at an appropriate level with the learners and their parents. Where there is diversity among practitioners in a setting, that is where there are bilingual practitioners, this makes it easier for them to draw on one another's expertise and experiences for the benefit of every learner, especially those with EAL.

In a more homogeneous setting, it is advantageous to reach out to local communities to widen this experience for learners with EAL in enriching the curriculum, but managing this can be challenging in terms of the time and resources required. Next we explore leadership and management in the context of Early Years.

Distinguishing between leadership and management

Leadership is about the bigger picture of change and influence, and management is about the day-to-day tasks to turn the setting's vision into reality. So we are interested in understanding how leaders in multi- and mono-cultural Early Years settings build individual and organisational capability and how they lead with values, such as equity, fairness, respect and tolerance (Bell and Stevenson, 2006: 143), which underpin their vision.

As mentioned throughout the book, every setting is different with different contexts, background and history, so each may 'interpret, articulate and implement' the concepts of diversity and equity differently (Bell and Stevenson, 2006: 143). We are reminded by Gold, cited in Coleman and Glover (2010), that there may be conflicting values and therefore can we ever be sure if all leaders hold the same values? Gold goes on to say that 'values are implicit in all of us . . . they guide every decision we make, even if we are not aware of this' (2010: 25). So the challenge for leadership is how best they align different values in the interest of learners and excellent educational practice.

The work of Lumby *et al.* (2005) showed how leaders in urban and rural organisational settings found it challenging to manage diverse staff. But with a diverse workforce, they found that the leadership required the use of some different intercultural skills and competences that were not so evident where there were fewer staff from different backgrounds. Lumby and Coleman's (2007) critique of diversity and equality in educational settings offers a refreshing viewpoint, stating that supporting diversity amongst leadership may result in a 'redistribution of power' that may be uncomfortable for a dominant group (p. 79). To give this chapter some Early Years context, we begin by looking at some of the differences between leadership and management (see Table 8.1).

In the context of Early Years this means that practitioners need to consider themselves as leaders of learning first and foremost, which necessitates maximising their expertise and experiences for the benefit of their learners. In relation to leading and managing learning for learners with EAL, it means providing the highest quality educational experiences through thorough planning, preparation and assessment. We turn next to reviewing some ideas about how leadership and management are applied to learners with EAL, as illustrated by Table 8.2.

This table shows that leadership is about selling the vision through skills that enable, influence and persuade people to do the right thing. Management is about maximising personal skills and abilities to deliver high quality educational experiences for the learners. The key thought is how practitioners come to a consensus regarding agreement about vision setting, for example, asking what is the value of educational learning experience for a given setting. If one is not in agreement with another during discussion, how will each listen to the other's views to reach an agreed idea? To get everyone to agree with each other is not so easy, so do not feel deflated if it does not work the first

Table 8.1 Suggested differences between leaders and managers in Early Years

Managers in Early Years have been described as:	In contrast, leaders in Early Years have been described as:
• Guardians of the setting's aims, the process and the means of achieving them • Allocating the organisation's resources to achieve its aims • Normally cautious, seeking to preserve and strengthen the status quo • Involved in fundamental processes such as planning and budgeting, organising and controlling	• Having a responsibility to question what exists, consider alternatives, break new ground • Involved in the articulation of a mission and the means to achieve it • Responsible for creating a vision, the best strategy to achieve the vision and the ideal environment . . . which ultimately leads to the achievement of the vision

Table 8.2 The difference between leadership and management in Early Years

A Leader/Leadership Chaos/Dynamic	Application to learners with EAL	A Manager/ Management Safety/Security	Application to learners with EAL
Has an eye on the horizon	Sees the bigger picture on how learners with EAL make progress	Administers	Focused on daily activities for learners with EAL like target setting for progression, data analysis and deploying resources appropriately
Develops	Develops staff to meet the needs of learners with EAL through support	Maintains	Ensures high quality provision leads to high quality learner experience and attainment
Focuses on people	Understands the needs and wants of diverse group of practitioners	Focuses on systems and structure	Focused on meeting the needs of learners with EAL through having simple systems and processes that can be followed easily in place
Inspires trust	The behaviour and actions of a leader are important indicators that inspire trust	Relies on control	Makes opportunities for learners with EAL to be creative so that the learning is fun, safe and exciting
Has a long-range perspective	Keeping a mid- to long-term vision is crucial	Has short-range view	Short- to mid-term planning monitored and evaluated to ensure consistency of approach to learners with EAL
Innovates	Looks for opportunities to deploy resources to offer high quality, innovative and creative practice for learners with EAL	Asks how and when	Innovates and questions practice continually, and plans to offer support where necessary; this may involve teamworking or seeking specific skills of a bilingual practitioner
Asks why – and why not?	Innovates and questions practice continually, aspiring all to offer high quality teaching and learning for learners with EAL	Always has an eye on the bottom line	Supports learner-centred learning so as to provide the highest quality learning for learners with EAL
Challenges the status quo	Probes and questions to improve quality; does not shy away from asking hard questions about how best to meet the needs of learners with EAL	Challenges the team to work	Motivates and encourages collegiality in problem-solving to produce the highest quality learning resources and teaching and learning approaches
Is their own person	Has high emotional intelligence to understand the needs of diverse learners	Is a member of and a leader of a team	Has specific skills, knowledge and understanding such as bilingual skills

time! We have to learn to persevere. Therefore, maybe one challenge for Early Years settings is to do more of leadership and less of management, that is, to think bigger, to be more visionary, and to find more allies, which may be the domain of leadership activities. But Aubrey (2010: 13) suggests there may be reluctance to engage with concepts of leadership by those working in Early Years settings because the concept is so contested. She cites the work of Rodd (1996), suggesting that early childhood leadership literature is either based on anecdotes or presented as tips for leaders, rather than as research, as shown by Case study 8.1.

Case study 8.1

Nisha was an experienced Early Years practitioner and was responsible for all aspects of Early Years in a large primary setting. Her role (in addition to teaching) was to lead other practitioners in the setting and to make sure that it ran smoothly on a daily basis. When questioned about her roles and responsibilities, the following dialogue took place:

Q: Who leads Early Years in a given setting?
Meera: I do.
Q: What is your perceived role from a leadership perspective?
Meera: To make sure that all practitioners in the setting are implementing the EYFS to the best of their ability with the resources they need. I also have to make sure that assessment is conducted regularly and correctly to aid learner progress especially for learners with EAL.
Q: What strategies are used to support practitioners with EAL learners?
Meera: We use lots of visual resources, and practitioners come to me if they would like specific resources to support learners with EAL.

This dialogue shows that Nisha saw her role as an Early Years leader as being to make sure that the setting ran smoothly on a daily basis. She did not see her role from a leadership perspective, whereby she could discuss how the vision of the setting was demonstrated in practice for learners with EAL, or how she embedded and supported changes within the setting to benefit all learners and practitioners. Or indeed how she communicated with practitioners effectively or how she managed the Early Years team to ensure progress for all learners was evident.

Sood and Mistry (2011) have identified that much more cultural awareness and practical strategies are needed to put theory into practice in the Early Years settings they researched. There is a 'serious lack of leadership development' (Aubrey, 2010: 13), implying that many Early Years leaders may be 'significantly under-prepared' (ibid.) for their roles, especially in leading a multi-disciplinary team, which is a key feature of such settings. Next are two examples of the roles and jobs of different leaders emerging from a survey conducted by Aubrey (2010).

Early Years leader

Role: to provide opportunities for practitioners to develop; work with lead practitioner; work with curriculum leader; promote the professional development of practitioners; attend to individual needs of practitioners; play a leading role; undertake particular administrative tasks.

Integrated-centre setting leadership

Job: to deliver better outcomes for learners with EAL under five years old and their families; support different types of partnerships like home–setting and parent–governor board, for example, one setting developed a good project based on using resources from the nearby multicultural resource centre in creating an excellent learning environment within their own setting which had greater than 95 per cent minority ethnic learners.

The common verbs that appear in the role or jobs described are to do with managing, leading, developing, establishing and delivering. So leadership and management are very much linked to action and outcomes in some shape or form, like mentoring, coaching and support. In that respect, therefore, *every* practitioner is a leader/manager; an ambivalent attitude, suggesting that they are not, as appears to be evidenced in the study undertaken by Mistry and Sood (2011), is no longer credible.

It is more likely that emerging leaders need to find space and time to reflect on the perceptions and definitions of leadership, and more specifically, what skills and perspectives they bring to influence practice in a culturally diverse community. The new terminology describing leadership regardless of setting seems to be 'beginning leaders', 'competence leaders' and 'master leaders' (Aubrey, 2010), but whatever the label, leadership appears to be likened to navigating the rapids, with, it seems, only the best surviving when creating excellent learning environments for their learners with EAL!

So far, we have suggested that differences between leadership and management are sometimes unhelpful divides, but often in practice, practitioners do not necessarily make this distinction. However, a distinction can be made between the processes of leadership and of management. Leadership focuses on people and management is concerned with achieving results through others. However, the notion of leadership is playing a more important role because the current thinking is to act as teams, in more holistic ways, and this means leadership is about motivating and gaining practitioners' commitment and engagement with a vision for the future. Managers and leaders therefore need to continue to work with dignity and behaviours which are ethically driven.

Different approaches to leading and managing within a setting

There are various leadership and management models and styles that may be utilised when looking at educational settings. Depending on which model is used, they will show a different view of life in these settings, so we need to be cautious about which model to choose as none provides a complete picture (Sergiovanni, 1984), especially in relation to Early Years. So no one setting can be explained by using only a single approach, model or theory (Bush, 2003). There are many theories which can be linked to education, but two key areas are bureaucratic theories, where 'top-down' leadership is regarded as the central concept of effective management, and theories such as collegial, political, subjective and ambiguity theories (see Bush and West-Burnham, 1994). Each leader will promote learning in their setting differently depending on their context and the resources available to them, especially in meeting the specific language needs of learners with EAL. There are many examples in Ofsted reports that highlight good practice in supporting learners with EAL, such as deploying bilingual practitioners or using community members in translation of documentation or as interpreters or as volunteers in promoting classroom learning as partners or governors. Indeed, there are often vacancies for minority ethnic governors in some boroughs/counties, an area worth investigating further beyond the realms of this book. Let us briefly turn to the different models of leadership next.

Transformational leadership is one dominant model of leadership which focuses on developing and inculcating a vision of a preferred future for the school (Bush, 2003). The aim of this model is to promote and develop the instructional leadership capabilities of practitioners for promoting learning. Another model is instructional leadership which focuses on teaching and learning and on the behaviour of teachers in working with learners (Bush and Glover, 2002: 10). In terms of Early Years this model offers practitioners greater opportunity to define what the setting's mission is, whether it is a multicultural or monocultural setting and within this, manage the curriculum to best cater for the needs of learners with EAL, for example in an inclusive culture (Hallinger, 2011), but we are mindful that other models do exist.

Leadership for learning

Frost and Durrant (2002) suggest that practitioners should demonstrate high quality leadership for learning as mentors and coaches for other practitioners. They argue that practitioner-led development work can be 'radically transformed' (p. 13). Learning for the twenty-first century is changing with 'changing demographics of settings, the explosion of technology, and the rapid growth and change in knowledge requir[ing] individuals who can live with ambiguity, work flexibly, encourage creativity, and handle complexity' (Crow, 2001: 2). Therefore leadership will have to change to 'learning a new role' (Crow, 2001: 2). So we need to rethink what leadership means in terms of leadership for learners with EAL. This implies strengthening teaching and learning with visionary leadership based on commitment to values and conviction that learners will learn at high levels in an entrepreneurial spirit (Murphy and Schwarz, 2000).

As practitioners we need to start thinking of a holistic, rounded experience for our learners with EAL before we start tackling issues of what is effective learning for them. Different countries and cultures will have a different view of what education means. For some, it may come from allegiance to being passive, respectful and dutiful, as in China (Dimmock and Walker, 1998), or witnessing a more liberal approach of encouraging independent thinking and challenge, like in England. According to Lumby (2001: 5), learners prefer practitioners who show balance between discipline and friendliness and can help learners to advance through collaborative ways. This approach may suit learners with EAL more so than indigenous learners, as effective learning is dependent on a learner's relationship with the practitioner which in turn is key to their attitude towards learning (Stoll and Fink, 1996; Bowring-Carr and West-Burnham, 1997). We will return to leadership and learning for EAL later in the chapter.

How leadership can be applied in Early Years settings

We have looked at the wider debate about leadership and management as a concept and now turn our attention to its applicability in these settings. The unique aspect of the Early Years workforce is that it comprises a wide range of practitioners, each with different experience, training and qualifications. Solly (2003) highlights the number of young and sometimes inexperienced practitioners working in the sector and emphasises that the specific leadership context is multi-professional, primarily female, and socially and culturally varied. Traditionally leadership has been associated with individual skills characteristics and personal qualities in the leader which are essential to the contextual nature of the environment (Nivala and Hujala, 2002). It is often suggested that the role of leaders is to give a sense of direction to the setting and practitioners (Fullan, 2001), and this vision-setting is a crucial leadership function. But we have to be careful that this vision-setting takes consideration of multiple views and is not driven by a single leader or small group. Bruce (2010) warns us of the danger of this single-minded approach and, rather, to be mindful of 'people's different perspectives and experiences' (p. 359).

The challenge remains of how best to capture the views of the wider community (families and their learners) in creating an inclusive vision. Currently in England the National College for School Leadership is actively promoting development opportunities (DfE, 2013) for Early Years leaders. As part of its Community Leadership Strategy, it has introduced the first national programme to address the needs of leaders within multi-agency Early Years settings as it recognises that leadership has a clear distinctive focus (NCSL, 2005).

By reflecting on this chapter and the reflective questions at the end, greater understanding of and reflection on the roles and responsibilities of an Early Years leader in supporting the learning of learners with EAL is likely to occur. So, for example, if an Early Years leader talks about managing the aims of the setting, this may mean looking at how the EYFS is organised in terms of areas of learning for various topics that maximise the learning opportunities for learners with EAL. It may also mean looking at how planning happens for both indoor and outdoor learning, who is involved in this process, how the planning is linked to develop coherence of the learning for learners with EAL and how the team works to gather evidence of learning for their assessment. By reflecting on these questions, we hope the practitioner gains a better understanding of the leadership and management concepts. They may also find there is much overlapping of roles and activities.

Coleman (2011) has developed a useful notion about leadership and has coined the term 'resourceful leadership'. He suggests that the most effective leaders of learners' services are resourceful, and that the most highly effective leaders of learners' services consistently display a common set of eight behaviours in their leadership practice, which collectively is best described as resourceful. So what does resourceful mean in the context of Early Years supporting learning for learners with EAL? It means:

- making the most of human and physical resources in a setting; for example, deploying a Gujerati-speaking practitioner to tell a story in Gujerati and English where predominant learners are Gujerati speaking (or another predominant language);
- expanding the resource base further by auditing what resources are additionally needed for new topics that will promote excellent learning environments for

learners with EAL; for example, buying in books that show different kinds of build-ings around the world when looking at Understanding the World in the EYFS (DfE, 2014);

- utilising both internal and external resources that highlight the importance of the outdoor environment; for example, using sand and water trays inside and outside with different resources to show how resources can be adapted.

Coleman (2011) suggests that a resourceful leader exhibits a number of core behaviours as suggested in Table 8.3. However, we have adapted these to fit the context of Early Years, and have taken them one step further to include some examples for learners with EAL.

Table 8.3 shows that a resourceful leader uses a range of behaviours to work through others to achieve the best results possible. The important point about these experiences is how the leaders turn their learning to make a positive difference to learners with EAL and, arguably, to other members of the setting community (such as parents), not forget-ting those who can be isolated. There is more emphasis now on the impact of learning on learners, as well as on value for money. We firmly believe that all leaders need to continually learn so that they are seen to be good role models for others in order to con-tinue to promote excellent learning environments for EAL learners.

Role of a leader in promoting high quality learning experiences for EAL learners

The role of a good leader is to establish a vision for the setting, use her/his influence to encourage others to share that vision and then help to create the conditions needed to turn the vision of Early Years into reality. Table 8.4 illustrates how a good leader can achieve this.

The particular style of leadership will depend on the personal characteristics and expe-rience of the leader and this may need to be adapted over time to respond to changing situations and challenges. Leadership does not happen in isolation as there is normally a team approach in Early Years settings. Good interpersonal skills (such as being able to listen, being able to talk to different people at different levels) are therefore of paramount importance, and the ability to inspire trust and confidence is also an essential attribute of a good leader.

It appears then that the primary role of the leader is to be responsible for organising the people and resources that will translate the setting's vision into high quality services for all learners and their parents. This involves deploying effective leadership knowledge, understanding, ability, skills, emotional intelligence and competencies and developing a wide range of management skills for effective outcomes. This background knowledge needed by an effective Early Years leader includes an understanding of:

- what constitutes good practice for the learning and development of learners with EAL;
- how to implement the welfare requirements of the EYFS for learners with EAL;
- the legislative requirements covering childcare, employment and premises such as the outdoor environment impacting learners with EAL specifically;
- the implementation of health and safety legislation, including food safety, especially at snack time for learners with EAL;

Table 8.3 Coleman's (2011) resourceful leader attributes linked to developing learning for learners with EAL

Core behaviours	In the context of Early Years	For learners with EAL
1. The ability to simplify	To translate the EYFS into practice	To select the most relevant educational aims to meet the specific needs of learners with EAL such as more language repetition with supporting resources in context (Communication and Language, EYFS, 2014)
2. Displaying a focus on results and outcomes	To have a clear understanding of the Foundation Stage Profile	Tracking the progress of EAL learners through various assessments in smaller steps, the focus being the highest level of attainment for each learner with EAL; consider using all practitioners in producing bilingual or multilingual resources to raise awareness such as words in different languages for greetings or key words that support assessment
3. Willingness and ability to learn continuously	To adapt practice to changing government priorities	By networking with parents of EAL learners to understand the context that learners have come from, or by going on training courses associated with meeting the needs of diverse learners; where bilingual learners are considered as an asset, learn a language (or key words) from them to benefit them
4. Openness to possibilities	To listen to the advice of others, and also by going into different Early Years settings to observe good practice	To observe different strategies of how the needs of learners with EAL are being met elsewhere in similar settings; then look for creative ways to provide high quality learning experiences for learners with EAL, for example, by encouraging family members of learners with EAL to engage in all stages of curriculum planning, implementation and evaluation
5. Personal resilience and tenacity	Being flexible when planning changes	Adjusting planning as and when necessary to make it more creative using visual resources to support EAL learners; for example, the use of puppets to make story time more interactive
6. Demonstrating a belief in their team and people	The ability to create and sustain commitment across a system; for example, make sure that all in the team have the same shared vision for all learners	By deploying practitioners who have specific knowledge, understanding and skills of wider cultural needs of learners with EAL; for example, drawing on the expertise of other practitioners in the setting who have more experience of working with learners with EAL
7. The ability to collaborate	Take ideas on board from all practitioners in the setting	Working with local communities to promote the highest quality learning experiences for learners with EAL; for example, celebrate the linguistic diversity of the setting through use of, e.g. music, dance, posters with simple words

Table 8.4 How leadership features help develop learners with EAL

Do what?	How?	For learners with EAL
Be a source of inspiration to colleagues and the 'guardian of the vision' of the setting	Through sharing ideas of good practice and leading by example	Use the strengths of the practitioners to best cater for their needs, e.g. forging links with local communities to acquire resources
Work hard to establish good two-way communication with members of the Early Years team	Through discussions to help them feel that their contribution to success is valued and respected	Tell a story in two languages (or more if necessary) with support from other practitioners in the team to help make learning accessible to learners with EAL
Involve others in the decision-making process	By ensuring that all practitioners understand what has to be done and are aware of their role in the process	Ask bilingual practitioners to help prepare materials to be sent home to the families of learners with EAL
Monitor progress through assessment and achievement	Model good practice	Jointly assess learners in different areas of learning in order to evaluate their conceptual understanding as well as their language
Provide personal encouragement	By finding ways to recognise and reward good performance	Through modelling their own practice as excellent teachers of learning; bilingual learners can help

- child protection legislation and local guidelines and procedures applicable for learners with EAL specifically;
- equality and inclusion, for learners, parents and staff; and
- finance and budgeting to best meet the needs of learners with EAL.

In summary, leadership's thrust in essence is to translate the setting's vision into high quality services for all, learners and practitioners. Excellent leadership is centred on being a lead learner in oneself, passion for learning and learners, and building effective relationships using personal influence, persuasion, tact and trust. Let us briefly look next at effective leadership skills in light of Early Years practice.

An effective leader would also benefit from utilising the following skills:

- Strategic thinking – meaning an ability to see the big picture but also to keep track of all the smaller actions and initiatives which come together to deliver the overall vision of the setting, especially when it comes to meeting the needs of learners with EAL.
- Good organisation and planning in all areas of learning including inclusion for learners with EAL – being able to deal with issues in a structured and methodical way and seeing projects through to completion.

- Effective communication – an ability to pass on information and ideas to a variety of different audiences in a clear and understandable way, especially for the parents of new EAL arrivals.
- Good time management – the self-discipline to plan ahead, structure the working day and week well for all practitioners, and keep to deadlines.
- Sensible delegation to suit the strengths of team members – the confidence to pass responsibility on to the most appropriate member of the team and then monitor that delegated tasks have been completed.
- Financial awareness – an understanding of the technicalities of managing a budget and the requirements of financial probity.
- Interpersonal skills – an ability to act at different times as leader, motivator, mentor, coach or authority figure – along with the skills to carry out each of these roles well, especially for learners who have EAL and their parents who may not be as confident with communication.
- Self-awareness and self-confidence – an awareness of personal strengths and weaknesses and the ability to use these effectively in the workplace.
- A positive attitude to change – the maturity to reflect on, and learn from, previous experience.

In brief, good practice of inclusion of learners with EAL shows that those practitioners with a higher level of empathy and a wider awareness of the cultural needs of their learners with EAL and parents will succeed more. This means that if practitioners are bilingual, it will enable them to utilise their personal and professional experience to support learners with EAL and their families (Devarakonda, 2013: 88). The challenge for leaders is to find practitioners with appropriate knowledge and skills to deliver appropriately to meet the needs of learners with EAL and, importantly perhaps, also their families who may speak different languages.

Additional examples of recommendations for leaders to support learners with EAL (DfES, 2007) include:

- make better use of setting's data to identify and tackle the particular needs of EAL learners and to set appropriately challenging targets;
- analyse closely the writing of learners with EAL to identify the specific difficulties they face when writing in English;
- make sure that language policies and schemes of work reflect the specific linguistic needs of learners with EAL, at both the early and more advanced stages of language acquisition;
- clarify the role of practitioners outside the setting to deploy them effectively in order to focus on the specific needs of learners with EAL;
- provide direct instruction about specific features of writing and give detailed feedback to learners with EAL on their writing;
- build on learners' cultural and linguistic experiences by encouraging them to talk about writing done at home and by forging closer links with families to understand the ways they try to support their EAL learners with writing at home;
- introduce learners to good quality texts and a wide range of genres and styles of writing, so that learners with EAL experience the full diversity of written texts, as recommended by the EYFS (DfE, 2014); and

- ensure that practitioners are fully aware of how to meet the specific linguistic needs of learners with EAL by making available key research and relevant training.

Managerial effectiveness is about performance and it is to do with how people achieve and how people behave. To measure effectiveness it is necessary to understand and define both sides of the equation, that is, inputs (skills and behaviour) and outputs (results). So put simply, 'effective managers get the things done that they are expected to get done' (Armstrong, 2009: 25). It is important to understand that management is *not* just about management; it also involves leadership! So Early Years leaders provide guidance and support to their practitioners through leadership and performance management processes (such as agreeing roles and expectations, providing feedback). They also act as coaches and mentors, advising, helping practitioners to learn by doing. The variety of these activities shows the complexity of the role and why the work of managers is often fragmented and confused with leadership, hence stating above that the two terms are highly contested with multiple meanings. The following scenario looks at aspects of both leadership and management in Early Years (DCSF, 2011).

Scenario 1

This Early Years setting has about 57 per cent of learners with EAL, many of whom need considerable support in developing their skills in speaking and writing English. Most EAL learners make sound progress through the setting because of the supportive and caring atmosphere provided, and because the Early Years leader maintains sound systems to track learners' progress as they develop their language skills. However, many of these learners could make better progress with more focused and better managed provision. The learners with EAL are taught to a satisfactory level overall but there are areas for development. The information from assessment is not shared between practitioners in the setting and there are no specific targets derived from them for practitioners to use in planning, particularly literacy. There are two bilingual practitioners employed to give language support to pupils throughout the setting, together with practitioners from outside the setting. The practitioners give sensitive and effective mother-tongue support to the youngest learners in the setting, and help them to develop a survival vocabulary when they first arrive.

   Support for older learners is not always as effective, particularly in whole-group sessions when not all of these practitioners participate in the introduction to activities. In many activities, learners are effectively encouraged to listen to their practitioners who provide them with good role models of speaking. In most areas of learning, they use good examples of vocabulary that is specific to the planned learning and construct sentences to develop understanding of English. Effective questioning often stimulates learners' interest, but opportunities to develop language through articulating clear answers with correct vocabulary and appropriate sentence structures are regularly missed when practitioners accept limited answers from the learners with EAL. This scenario therefore shows the need for high expectations by practitioners and to ensure they continue to offer the best learning experiences for learners with EAL through tracked data analysis.

Leadership and pedagogy

Effective, imaginative, exciting and problem-solving teaching is the foundation of all learning in the Early Years. As practitioners, the most important thing that we do is to teach at the highest level we can. With good subject knowledge, good questioning skills and good setting organisation come excellent leadership capabilities. We are all leaders of learning and of teaching. Excellent leaders make things happen by setting a clear vision for learning and excellent teaching, and the management task is to ensure that teaching and learning does not remain poverty stricken. As excellent leaders, they have to put the magic into teaching and know what makes learning effective and of world-class status as envisioned by the Secretary of State for Education. We need to know some of the theories of learning so that we can plan effectively taking account of individual differences, especially for those learners with EAL. High expectation is the *raison d'être* of all practitioners who teach.

As leaders, we need to know what makes effective learning, and use this data to further improve pedagogy and progression for our learners. As we know, there are different forms of intelligences (Goleman, 1996); we also know there are different types of leadership styles that motivate and inspire practitioners. This implies that we continue to provide learners with EAL with different approaches, different leadership styles, and different teaching and learning opportunities, so that they can see the patterns. Early Years is a key period in developing the capacity for learning and leadership for learning of learners with EAL as an essential driver for us. Turning briefly to the twenty-first century, leaders will have to take a different approach to managing the needs of diverse learning communities, and therefore the role of education leadership is to help practitioners achieve this change. There are also political and cultural barriers to change requiring links with minority ethnic groups to gain a better understanding and awareness of their learners' needs and aspirations. The technological revolution is changing power relations, through opening knowledge and communications and changing the way society and the economy function (Lumby, 1997). We believe that Early Years practitioners have the ability and responsibility to help shape the direction of education, especially for learners with EAL, much earlier.

Summary

In summary, this chapter aimed to develop a deeper conceptual understanding of the contested nature of leadership and management in Early Years, and the normative and artificial divide between the two terms that becomes apparent. But to explain practice in the Early Years settings, we have presented the notions of leadership and management separately. We have endeavoured to use the evidence and theory considered to underpin the practicalities in these settings and have suggested that it is vital to link the understanding of leadership, learning and equity. Leadership and management roles and responsibilities have the dual role of ensuring organisational strategies align with the operational aspects requiring a shared philosophy and awareness of the wider political, social, cultural and educational context. Various leadership styles were analysed, with the resourceful leadership model considered to be one contemporary approach worthy of further critique and development. Diversity management is a challenge, as is the management of high quality educational experiences for all learners, and in particular, taking cognisance of promoting and creating excellent quality learning environments for learners with EAL.

Reflective questions

- Observe a leader in action. Make a diary and reflect on what makes them an excellent leader and why?
- How do leaders/managers create excellent pedagogical learning environments for learners with EAL?
- A resourceful leader has many qualities. Reflect on which ones work for a particular context and why?

References

Armstrong, M. (2009) *Armstrong's handbook of management and leadership: a guide to managing for results*. 2nd edn. London: Kogan Page.

Aubrey, C. (2010) *Leading and managing in the Early Years*. 2nd edn. London: Sage.

Bell, L. and Stevenson, H. (2006) Citizenship and social justice: developing education policy in multi-ethnic schools, in L. Bell and H. Stevenson (eds), *Education policy: process, themes and impact*. London: Routledge.

Bowring-Carr, C. and West-Burnham, J. (1997) *Effective learning in schools*. London: Pitman.

Bruce, T. (ed.) (2010) *Early childhood: a guide for students*. London: Sage.

Bush, T. (2003) *Theories of educational leadership and management*. 3rd edn. London: Sage.

Bush, T. and Glover, D. (2002) *School leadership: concepts and evidence*. Nottingham: National College for School Leadership.

Bush, T. and West-Burnham, J. (1994) *The principles of educational management*. Harlow: Longman.

Coleman, A. (2011) Resourceful leadership: how directors of children's services lead to improved outcomes for children. BELMAS Annual International Conference 2011, 8–10 July 2011, Wyboston Lakes, Bedfordshire, UK.

Coleman, M. and Glover, D. (2010) *Educational leadership and management: developing insights and skills*. Maidenhead: Open University Press and McGraw-Hill Education.

Conteh, J. (2012) *Teaching bilingual and EAL learners in primary schools*. London: Sage.

Crow, G. M. (2001) *School leader preparation: a short review of the knowledge base*. NCSL Research Archive, www.ncsl.org.uk (accessed June 2012).

DCSF (2011) *Supporting children learning EAL*, www.standards.dcsf.gov.uk/NationalStrategies (accessed April 2014).

Department for Education and Skills (DfES) (2007) *Excellence and enjoyment: learning and teaching for bilingual children in the primary years: teaching units to support guided sessions for writing in English as an Additional Language* (pilot material) 00068-2007FLR-EN Primary National Strategy, www.standards.dfes.gov.uk (accessed April 2014).

Department for Education (DfE) (2013) National College for Teaching and Leadership, www.education.gov.uk/ (accessed April 2014).

Department for Education (DFE) (2014) *Statutory framework for the Early Years Foundation Stage (EYFS)*. London: DFE.

Devarakonda, C. (2013) *Diversity and inclusion in early childhood*. London: Sage.

Dimmock, C. and Walker, A. (1998) Comparative educational administration: developing a cross-cultural conceptual framework. *Educational Administration Quarterly*, 34(4): 558–95.

Edberg, H. (2013) Gandhi's 10 rules for changing the world, www.dailygood.org/story/466/gandhi-s-10-rules-for-changing-the-world-henrik-edberg/ (accessed May 2014).

Frost, D. and Durrant, J. (2002) Teachers as leaders: exploring the impact of teacher-led development work. *School Leadership and Management*, 22(2): 143–61.

Fullan, M. (2001) *Leading in a culture of change*. San Francisco, CA: Jossey-Bass.

Goleman, M. (1996) *Emotional intelligence*. London: Bloomsbury.

Hallinger, P. (2011) Leadership for learning: lessons from 40 years of empirical research. *Journal of Educational Administration*, 49(2): 125–42.

Lumby, J. (1997) The learning organisation, in T. Bush and D. Middlewood (eds), Managing people in education. London: Paul Chapman.

Lumby, J. (2001) Framing teaching and learning in the 21st century, in D. Middlewood and N. Burton (eds), *Managing the curriculum*. London: Sage, pp. 1–14.

Lumby, J. and Coleman, M. (2007) *Leadership and diversity: challenging theory and practice in education*. London: Sage.

Lumby, J., Harris, A., Morrison, M., Muijs, D., Sood, K., Glover, D., Wilson, M., with Briggs, A. R. J. and Middlewood, D. (2005) *Leadership development and diversity in the learning and skills sector*. London: LSDA.

Mistry, M. and Sood, K. (2011) Raising standards for pupils who have English as an Additional Language (EAL) through monitoring and evaluation of provision in primary schools, www.tandfonline.com/loi.rett20 (accessed March 2014).

Murphy, J. and Schwarz, P. (2000) Reinventing the principalship: report of a task force on the principalship, in *School leadership for the 21st century initiative*. Washington, DC: Institute for Educational Leadership at University of Lincoln.

National College for School Leadership (2005) *Community leadership*, www.ncsl.org.uk/community_leadership/communityleadership-index.cfm (accessed March 2014).

Nivala, V. and Hujala, E. (eds) (2002) *Leadership in early childhood education: cross-cultural perspectives*. Oulu, Finland: Department of Educational Sciences and Teacher Education, Early Childhood Education, University of Oulu, http://herkules.oulu.fi/isbn9514268539/isbn9514268539.pdf (accessed March 2013).

Rodd, J. (1996) Towards a typology of leadership for the early childhood professional of the 21st century. *Early Childhood Development and Care*, 120: 119–26.

Sergiovanni, T. (1984) Leadership and excellence in schooling. *Educational Leadership*, 41(5): 4–13.

Solly, K. (2003) What do early years leaders do to maintain and enhance the significance of the early years? A paper on a conversation with Kathryn Solly held at the Institute of Education on 22 May 2003.

Sood, K. and Mistry, M. (2011) English as an Additional Language: is there a need to embed cultural values and beliefs in institutional practice? *Education 3–13*, 39(2): 203–15.

Stoll, L. and Fink, D. (1996) *Changing our schools*. Buckingham: Open University.

Glossary

Areas of learning – the prime and specific areas of learning in the EYFS

Communication – how individuals engage and respond with one another to express meaning and understanding

Early Years – age phase of learners from birth to five years old (0–5) in England

Early Years Foundation Stage (EYFS) – curriculum for learners aged 0–5 in all government-registered settings in England

English as an Additional Language (EAL) – learners who are learning English in addition to their first or home language(s)

e-profile – an electronic profile tool used to gather evidence for learners aged 0–5 to track their progress against the Early Learning Goals in the EYFS

Ethnic Minority Achievement Grant (EMAG) – a practitioner who leads on working with EAL learners in settings

Formative assessment – collection of evidence that feeds into the assessment process for analysis

Globalisation in Early Years – educational opportunities, experiences and learning that stem from beyond the setting

Inclusive culture – to create opportunities for learners to have a broad range of experiences in their learning that stems from all backgrounds and cultures

Language – the main form of communication between individuals or groups

Learner(s) – includes all children and pupils

Monolingual – practitioners and learners who are only able to speak and understand one language

New EAL arrivals – those learners who have come from abroad or a different setting in England and have EAL

Office for Standards in Education (Ofsted) – watchdog for regulating standards of education in England

Parents – also includes carers and guardians

Partnerships – between parents and practitioners in a setting, between practitioners in different settings, between settings and outside agencies

Pedagogy – the science or art of teaching

Planning cycle – a framework used to help support practitioners with their planning

Practitioners – comprises all staff in a setting such as teachers, teaching assistants, nursery nurses, key workers, bilingual staff, managers/leaders

Setting – includes lower schools, Early Years in primary schools, nurseries, playgroups, day care centres

Special Educational Needs Co-ordinator (SENCO) – a practitioner who leads on working with learners who have additional needs

Summative assessment - results gained at the end of specific assessments (such as Early Learning Goals)

Support agencies – such as Local Authority Advisors, Language Support Team workers, Speech and Language Therapists

Systematic Synthetic Phonics (SSP) – way of coding and decoding sound to support reading and writing in Early Years

Index

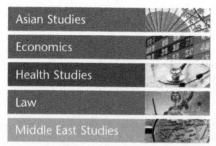